THE

BARAKAH MORNING

A Still, Strengthening Beginning to the Day

Railu Mustapha-Tiamiyu

ISBN 978-1-914286-33-9

Published by **Tranquility Hub Limited**

Printed in the United Kingdom

Typeset in a custom blend of serif and humanist fonts designed for long-form reading comfort.

Qur'anic āyat and prophetic narrations are cited from authenticated, classical sources and presented with full reverence.

The content herein is intended for spiritual inspiration and personal development. It does not replace the guidance of qualified scholars.

First Edition — 2025

www.tranquilityhub.com

Dedication

To the One who guided my heart
when my mornings felt heavy
and opened doors I could not see.

To those I love
who carried me through the quiet tests
no one else ever knew.

And to you —
the one who picked up this book
because your heart hoped for something better.

May Allah fill your mornings with barakah,
your days with ease,
and your life with a clarity
that comes only from Him.

"O Allah, bless my Ummah in their early mornings."

— Tirmidhi

Author's Note

Every book begins long before the first word is written.
This one began in the quiet moments —
the mornings that slipped away,
the days that felt heavy,
the prayers whispered with a tired heart,
and the longing for a life anchored in clarity, purpose, and nearness to Allah.

I wrote this book because I needed it first.

I needed a way to reclaim my mornings.
I needed a rhythm that softened my heart instead of hardening it.
I needed a structure that brought barakah back into my time,
and a daily practice that reminded me that Allah is near —
not abstractly, but practically, intimately, and powerfully near.

What you hold in your hands is not a manual written from theory.
It is a blueprint built from lived experience, from Islamic tradition,
and from a deep desire to make spiritual consistency feel possible again.

This book is for you if your mornings have felt scattered,
if your heart has felt distant,
if your days slip by faster than you can hold them,
or if you simply want to begin again —
with Allah at the centre.

My intention is that every page gently pulls you back to what matters:
the remembrance of Allah,

the stillness of the early hours,
the sacred structure the Prophet ﷺ taught us,
and the barakah that unlocks when you turn your face to the dawn with sincerity.

May this book meet you where you are.
May it uplift you, calm you, and accompany you.
May it help you build a morning that strengthens your īmān,
stabilises your heart, and fills your life with the quiet, steady light of barakah.

And may Allah make every word in these pages a witness for you,
not against you,
on the Day when nothing else matters.

Yā Allah, bless the one who reads this.
Bless their mornings, their time, their heart, their home,
and the path that leads them back to You.

Ameen.

Preface

There is a moment in every believer's life when they realise something essential:

Life works differently when Allah is at the centre.

Time feels lighter.
Decisions feel clearer.
Challenges feel softer.
Provision arrives in ways that defy logic.
And the heart moves with a steadiness it never had before.

But reaching that place — that state of inner alignment — requires a doorway.
For centuries, the early Muslims agreed on where that doorway begins:

the morning.

Not simply waking up early,
not just performing tasks efficiently,
but entering the morning with intention, remembrance, structure, and presence.

This book is built on a simple truth:
Your morning is the root of your entire life.
If you transform your morning, you transform everything that grows from it.

The Barakah Morning is not a productivity system borrowed from modern culture.
It is a return to the Prophetic rhythm —
a rhythm that strengthens īmān, calms the heart, protects time, and brings clarity to the mind.

In these pages, you will not only *learn* the habits that unlock barakah —
you will *experience* them.

Each chapter is designed to be:

- spiritually grounded
- psychologically practical
- emotionally accessible
- and easy to integrate into real life

This is not a book to read once and place on a shelf.
It is a manual to return to whenever the heart needs rebalancing,
whenever the soul feels heavy,
whenever life becomes loud.

My hope is that you use these mornings
to rebuild your relationship with Allah,
to reclaim control over your time and attention,
and to construct a life that feels meaningful again.

May the Barakah Morning become your anchor —
a daily reminder that Allah is near,
that your du'ā' is heard,
that your effort is seen,
and that your day can unfold with beauty when you begin it with Him.

Welcome to the journey.
Welcome to the dawn.
Welcome to the morning where everything changes.

Sources & Inspirations

The foundations of this book are rooted in the Qur'an, the authentic Sunnah, and the enduring wisdom preserved by generations of scholars. Whatever clarity appears in these pages is a reflection of that noble legacy.

I wish to acknowledge the public teachings and reflections that shaped the core structure of *The Barakah Morning*. In particular:

Shaykh Samih Jad — whose talk on early-morning discipline and spiritual focus formed the backbone of the practical routine in this book.

Sheikh Assim Al-Hakeem — whose explanations of the morning adhkār enriched the spiritual dimension woven throughout these chapters. May Allah reward them generously and place light in their efforts.

Classical Islamic references throughout this work draw upon authenticated sources, including:

- The Qur'an
- Sahih al-Bukhari
- Sahih Muslim
- The works of Imām an-Nawawī
- Insights from Ibn al-Qayyim and other early scholars

This book emerged from their guidance, not as a replacement for it, but as a humble attempt to help modern readers live the barakah these scholars pointed us toward.

Any benefit in this work is from Allah alone; any shortcomings are mine.

How to Use This Book

Before you begin implementing anything, **read this book all the way through once**.

This first reading is not for action — it is for **orientation**.
It allows you to grasp the full vision, the flow of the habits, and how each practice fits into a larger barakah-based framework.

Once you have a clear grasp of what the book is about, return to the beginning and begin implementation — one habit at a time.

This is a book you first **orient yourself with**, then **live**.

Once you return for practice, do not rush.
This is not a book to skim or consume quickly.
It is a book to live with — slowly, deliberately, and with intention.

Each chapter is designed to recalibrate one part of your morning,
one part of your heart,
and one layer of your relationship with Allah.

Read it the way transformation happens:
quietly, consistently, and with sincerity.

1. Take One Habit at a Time

When you return for implementation, begin with one habit only.

Read it fully. Pause. Reflect.
Allow the idea to settle before moving forward.

True change does not come from accumulation —
it comes from **integration**. Small, sincere steps are how barakah enters.

2. Practice Before You Progress

Each habit builds upon the one before it. You are not meant to apply the entire system at once. Begin with a single practice and give it space to take root.

When you feel its presence shaping your morning,
only then move on.

This book rewards patience.

3. Use the Tools — They Are Part of the Method

This is not a theoretical book. It is intentionally practical.

You will find:

- morning routines
- checklists
- du'ā' sequences
- reflection prompts
- journaling and identity statements

Use them. Write in them. Return to them.

Adjust them to your season of life.
They are meant to support you — not constrain you.

4. Read with Gentleness, Not Pressure

This is not productivity driven by force.
It is productivity grounded in **barakah**.

Read at a pace that mirrors the mornings you are building:
calm, intentional, and present.

If a line resonates, stay with it.
If a section speaks to your heart, let it linger.

Growth happens where attention rests.

5. Expect Direction, Not Perfection

A barakah-filled morning is built gradually —
layer by layer, habit by habit.

Some days will feel focused.
Others may feel scattered.

Both are part of the process.

Return to Allah each morning.
Let the book guide your **direction**, not your speed.

6. Let the Book Grow with You

Your mornings will change.
Your responsibilities will shift.
Your heart will move through seasons.

Return to this book whenever you need realignment —
when you feel heavy, distracted, or disconnected.

Each return will reveal something new.

7. Remember the Purpose

This book is not about waking up early.
It is about waking up **aware**.

It is about beginning the day with remembrance, clarity, and trust —
placing Allah at the centre of your morning
so everything that follows carries His barakah.

Let each chapter be a doorway back to that reality.

Table of Contents

Author's Note 5

Preface 7

Sources & Inspirations 9

How to Use This Book 11

The Dawn That Transforms 21

1.1 The Most Overlooked Spiritual Reality of Our Time 22

1.2 Why This Book Exists 23

1.3 Why Fajr Changes Everything 24

1.4 The World Is Imitating the Sunnah — Without Knowing 26

1.5 If You Feel Far from Allah — This Is Where You Begin 27

1.6 What You Will Learn in This Book 28

1.7 A Promise from This Book 29

The Barakah Principle: 31

2.1 What Is Barakah? — A Practical Definition 31

2.2 The Sunnah View of Productivity 33

2.3 Why Barakah Appears in Some Lives and Not Others 33

2.4 Why Most Muslims Don't Experience Barakah Today 35

2.5 The Barakah Shift: What Changes When You Live "Aligned" 36

2.6 Barakah vs Productivity: Why Muslims Need a Different Model 37

2.7 The Morning Was Designed as a Spiritual Engine 38

2.8 The Core Principle of This Book 38

2.9 Why This Chapter Comes Before the Habits 39

2.10 A Dua to Begin This Journey 40

The Nine Habits Framework: 41

3.1 What This Framework Actually Is 41

3.2 The Core Insight: These Habits Are Not Equal 42

3.3 Why These Habits Are in This Order 44
3.4 Why You Don't Need to Start with All Nine 45
3.5 Why This System Works for Every Muslim 46
3.6 The Hidden Logic Behind the Framework 46
3.7 What You Can Expect as You Apply These Habits 47
3.8 What Comes Next 48
Habit 1 — Staying Awake After Fajr: The Morning Awakening Blueprint 49
4.1 — Why the Morning Determines Your Life 49
4.2 — Win the Night: The 3–2–1 Muslim Evening Routine 51
4.3 — Why Not Sleeping After Fajr Multiplies Blessings 59
4.4 — What Should You Actually DO After Fajr? 60
4.5 — Real-Life Muslim Morning Routines 61
4.6 — Your 30-Day Stay-Awake-After-Fajr Plan 88
4.7 — When You Struggle or Miss a Day 95
Habit 2 — Praise & Gratitude: 97
5.1 The Dawn of Gratitude 97
5.2 Counting Blessings — Not Burdens 98
5.3 The Science of Shukr 100
5.4 Daily Practice of Praise 100
5.5 Praise During Pressure 103
5.6 Reflection & Re-commitment 104
Habit 3 — Glorify Allah (Tasbīḥ & Dhikr) 106
6.1 Why Tasbīḥ Changes the State of the Heart 106
6.2 The Sunnah Dhikr Cycle — Morning, Evening, After Salah 108
6.3 The Deep Emotional Impact of "SubḥānAllāh" 110
6.4 Tasbīḥ as a Barakah Generator 111
6.5 Dhikr Routines for Every Personality Type 112

6.6 Reflection & Re-Commitment 114
Habit 4 — Recite Qur'an in the Morning 116
7.2 — The Three Pillars of a Qur'ānic Morning 118
7.3 — Your 10-Minute Qur'ān Plan —Beginner-Friendly 120
7.4 — The Qur'ān Ladder — Choose Your Level 120
7.5 — Reflection Prompts That Open the Heart 121
7.6 — Troubleshooting: When It Gets Hard 121
7.7 — Real Qur'ān Morning Templates for Real Lives 122
7.8 — Why This Habit Unlocks Barakah 123
Habit 5 — Send Ṣalawāt on the Prophet ﷺ 125
8.1 — Why Ṣalawāt Belongs in the Morning 125
8.2 — The Sunnah of Sending Ṣalawāt 127
8.3 — The 3 Forms of Morning Ṣalawāt 128
8.4 — Integrating Ṣalawāt Into the Barakah Morning Routine 129
8.5 — Ṣalawāt for Different Lifestyles 129
8.6 — Micro Moments for Ṣalawāt 130
8.7 — Troubleshooting: When It Feels Hard 131
8.8 — The Identity of "A Person of Ṣalawāt" 132
Habit 6 — Make Istighfār 133
9.1 — Why Istighfār Belongs in the Morning 134
9.2 — The Psychology of Istighfār 137
9.3 — The Three Types of Morning Istighfār 138
9.4 — Where Istighfār Fits in the Barakah Morning 140
9.5 — Real-Life Templates 143
9.6 — Micro-Moments of Istighfār 144
9.8 — The Identity of a Person of Istighfār 146
Habit 7 — Salatu Duḥā 148

10.1 — What Is Salatu Duḥā Exactly? 149
10.2 — Why This Prayer Matters for a Barakah Morning 149
10.3 — The Rizq Expansion Effect 150
10.4 — The Emotional Healing Effect 152
10.5 — Timing: The Optimal Window 152
10.6 — How to Pray Duḥā (Simple Guide) 154
10.7 — The Duḥā Mindset (Before You Begin) 156
10.8 — Real-Life Routines 156
10.9 — Troubleshooting 158
10.10 — The Identity Shift 159
Habit 8 — Make Du'ā' 160
11.1 — Why Du'ā' Hits Harder in the Morning 161
11.2 — The Structure of a Powerful Du'ā' 161
11.3 — The Prophet's Morning Du'ā' Blueprint 176
11.4 — The Four Types of Morning Du'ā' 179
11.5 — What to Ask For in the Morning (Dunya + Ākhirah) 182
11.6 — Du'ā' Templates For Different Seasons of Life 186
11.7 — The Barakah of Specificity 190
11.8 — The Du'ā' Journal — Optional but Incredibly Powerful 191
11.9 — What to Do When Du'ā' Feels Unanswered 193
11.10 — Troubleshooting 195
The Dua That Changes Your Day 200
Habit 9 — Practice Morning Ṣadaqah 211
13.1 — Why Morning Sadaqah? 211
13.2 — The Myth of "I Need Money to Give" 213
13.3 — The Four Levels of Morning Ṣadaqah 214
13.4 — The Connection Between Sadaqah and Rizq 216

13.5 — The Sadaqah Mindset 217
13.6 — Real-Life Morning Sadaqah Routines 219
13.7 — The "Morning Ṣadaqah Box" Method 221
13.8 — The Digital Barakah Method 223
13.9 — When You Need Something From Allah 224
13.10 — Troubleshooting 225
Morning, Every Day 228
14.1 — What Actually Changes When You Live This Way 229
14.2 — The Barakah Morning Is Not About Perfection 231
14.3 — Your New Identity: A Morning Servant of Allah 232
14.4 — Your 3 Non-Negotiables Going Forward 233
Identity Reset: Becoming the Person 236
15.1 The Islamic Identity Framework: "Be Before You Do" 236
"Actions are only by intentions." 237
15.2 The 4 Levels of Islamic Identity 237
15.3 The Biggest Identity Blockers 239
15.4 How to Build a Strong Islamic Identity — 5-Step Reset 239
15.5 The Day You Become Consistent — Identity Integration 241
15.6 Disruptions, Relapses, and 'Bad Days' 242
15.7 The Dhikr of Identity 242
15.8 Your New Identity Statement 243
Barakah-Based Productivity: Working 244
16.1 What Is "Barakah Productivity"? 244
16.2 Why Willpower Alone Fails Most Muslims 245
16.3 The 7 Barakah Multipliers 246
16.4 The Three Work Modes of a Muslim 249
16.5 The Barakah-Based Workday — Template 251

16.6 How to Work With Allah, Not For the Work 254
16.7 — Dhikr That Accelerates Work — Practical Guide 255
16.8 — The Niyyah Stack: Turning Every Task Into Worship 256
16.9 — Working From a State of Sakīnah 257
16.10 — The Barakah Review — End-of-Day Check-In 257
16.11 — The Promise of Barakah 258
The Jumu'ah Reset System: 259
17.1 — Why Friday Is the Ultimate Reset Day 259
17.2 The Friday Barakah Model 261
17.3 Pillar 1 — The Spiritual Reset 261
17.4 Pillar 2 — The Practical Reset 263
17.5 Pillar 3 — The Emotional Reset 266
17.6 The Jumu'ah Reset Checklist (Simple + Practical) 268
17.7 The Result of a Weekly Reset 268
Your 30-Day Transformation Plan 270
18.1 The Strategy Behind the 30-Day Plan — Why It Works 270
18.2 Week 1: Foundation — "Anchor the Dawn" 272
18.3 Week 2: Activation — "Let the Heart Wake Up" 273
18.4 Week 3: Expansion — "Move Into Action" 274
18.5 WEEK 4: INTEGRATION — 275
8.6 The Weekly Layout (Quick Summary) 276
18.7 The 30-Day Transformation Checklist 277
18.8 The Promise of 30 Days 277
The Lifelong Barakah Lifestyle 279
19.1 What It Means to Live With Barakah 279
19.2 The "Barakah Operating System" (BOS) 280
19.3 When Life Gets Busy, Chaotic, or Hard 282

CHAPTER 1

The Dawn That Transforms Your Dunya and Ākhirah

Why Fajr Is the Tniing Point of a Muslim's Life, Productivity, and Destiny

There is a moment in every believer's life when the heart whispers:
"I want more from my time.
More from my worship.
More from my purpose.
More from the life Allah gave me."

That moment almost always comes around Fajr.

Not at noon.
Not during a weekend reset.
Not in a motivational surge on a random evening.

It comes when the world is quiet, the soul is soft, and the caller calls:

> *"As-Ṣalātu khayrun min an-nawm."*
> Prayer is better than sleep.

This single declaration carries a truth that can reset a life:

Your morning is not just a time of day.

It is a divine opportunity.

It is the *gateway* to barakah — the type of growth, blessing, and ease that no productivity hack, planner, or self-help system can manufacture.

And it begins before the sun rises.

1.1 The Most Overlooked Spiritual Reality of Our Time

Modern life is engineered to destroy mornings.

Late nights.
Unlimited entertainment.
Cheap dopamine.
Stress.
Exhaustion.
Constant connectivity — but no real connection with Allah.

We wake up tired.
We wake up reactive.
We wake up chasing.
We wake up already behind.

But the Prophet ﷺ taught the exact opposite:

> *"O Allah, bless my Ummah in their early mornings."*
> — Tirmidhī

The early morning carries unique barakah, with its peak beginning after Fajr and extending until sunrise — a time the Prophet ﷺ specifically prayed for.

Barakah — divine multiplication — is not evenly distributed across the day.

It is placed where hearts are quiet, distractions are minimal, and the soul is most receptive.

Whether you are:

- a parent managing countless responsibilities,
- a student studying your way into the future,
- a professional juggling deadlines,
- or a believer trying to honour Allah while navigating a demanding world...

One truth stands: ***If you win the morning, you win your life.***

1.2 Why This Book Exists

This book was not written as an abstract spiritual reflection. It was written because Muslims today are drowning in:

- overwhelm
- spiritual disconnect
- unstructured days
- burnout
- procrastination
- self-doubt
- guilt over missed prayers
- lack of focus
- and a constant sense of "I should be doing better."

And the solution is not more pressure, more hustle, or more unrealistic expectations.

The solution is barakah.

This book gives you:

- a repeatable, sustainable routine
- based on nine prophetic habits
- proven by scholars, neuroscience, and lived experience
- grounded in revelation
- and refined through real Muslim lifestyles
- designed for modern pressures

This is not a book of theory. It is a field manual. A blueprint. A way of living.

By the end of this journey, you will have:

- a reshaped relationship with Fajr
- a peaceful night routine
- a purposeful morning routine
- a dhikr-based mindset
- a Qur'an-centred start to your day
- the ability to produce deep work with spiritual clarity
- a heart anchored in remembrance
- and the confidence to build a life aligned with Allah's pleasure

1.3 Why Fajr Changes Everything

Fajr is a spiritual fulcrum — a point where a small action shifts the entire direction of your life.

1 — Your Rizq Is Allocated in This Time

> *"This is the time where provisions are distributed."*
>
> — Shaykh Samih Jad

Is it literal?
Is it metaphysical?
Is it both?

Allah knows — but every Muslim who has lived a Fajr-centred life knows the truth:

Things simply go right.
Doors open.
Difficulties ease.
Barakah multiplies.

This is not superstition; it is a divine pattern.

2 — The Qur'an Hits Deeper in This Hour

> *"Indeed, the recitation at Fajr is witnessed."*
> — Sūrah Al-Isrā' Q17:78

Who witnesses it?
The angels.
Your soul.
Your destiny.
Allah knows best.

But the impact is unmistakable:
Qur'an recited after Fajr settles into the heart.
It rewires your day.
It strengthens discipline.
It lifts anxiety.
It becomes the anchor of your īmān.

3 — Your Whole Day Aligns Around Allah, Not Around Stress

Most people start their day with:

- emails
- alarms
- rushing
- social media
- panic
- obligations

But a believer who begins with Fajr starts with:

- clarity
- purpose
- centredness
- remembrance
- intention
- obedience
- barakah

This is a different *universe* of living.

1.4 The World Is Imitating the Sunnah — Without Knowing

Even non-Muslim CEOs have discovered what the Prophet ﷺ taught 1,400 years ago:

- Wake up at 4 am.
- Don't sleep after sunrise.
- Do deep work early.
- Exercise in the morning.
- Start the day in silence.
- Avoid your phone early.
- Sleep early.

But Muslims were given this wisdom long before Silicon Valley adopted it.

The Sunnah is the original productivity system.

We are not borrowing modern productivity — modern productivity is borrowing from us.

This book will show you how to return to the original source.

1.5 If You Feel Far from Allah — This Is Where You Begin

You may feel:

- inconsistent
- tired
- struggling with sin
- weak in worship
- overwhelmed
- spiritually dry
- behind in life

You are not alone. Every believer fights this battle. But here is the mercy of Allah:

You only need one habit to start transforming EVERYTHING.

And it begins with Fajr.

Start with the morning.
Even before you fix anything else.
Even before you solve every spiritual struggle.

Because the Qur'an, the Sunnah, and centuries of Muslim experience all confirm:

When the morning changes, the heart changes.
When the heart changes, life changes.

1.6 What You Will Learn in This Book

This book gives you a full blueprint of nine prophetic habits that unlock morning barakah:

Habit 1 — Stay Awake After Fajr
The core discipline that unlocks clarity, rizq, and focus.
Habit 2 — Praise and Gratitude (Al-Ḥamd)
A neurological and spiritual shift into a barakah mindset.
Habit 3 — Tasbīḥ & Dhikr (SubḥānAllāh)
The words that align your inner state with divine Tranquility.
Habit 4 — Qur'an Recitation
The habit that fills your morning with light.
Habit 5 — Ṣalawāt upon the Prophet ﷺ
A spiritual key that brings mercy, ease, and answered prayers.
Habit 6 — Istighfār
The cleansing that unlocks success and removes invisible barriers.
Habit 7 — Duḥā Prayer
The prayer of provision and upliftment.
Habit 8 — Practical Du'ā & Tawakkul
Turning your daily goals into worship.
Habit 9 — Morning Charity & Spending
The habit that attracts barakah faster than anything else.

And alongside that, you will master:

- the 3-2-1 Night Routine

- the Fajr-Aligned Daily Schedule
- the Morning Dhikr Roadmap
- the Barakah-Based Productivity System
- templates, checklists, and routines for every lifestyle

This book is not a lecture. It is a transformation manual.

1.7 A Promise from This Book

You do not need to change your entire life. You only need to change your morning — and Allah changes the rest.

> *"And whoever brings themselves close to Me by a handspan, I come to them an arm's length..."*
>
> — Hadith Qudsī

Every small act counts.
Every effort is seen.
And Allah never leaves a sincere seeker empty-handed.

You are about to begin a journey.

Not of speed.
Not of force.
Not of pressure.

But a journey of returning to the rhythm Allah designed for you.

A life of barakah.
A life of clarity.
A life of purpose.

When the morning becomes your anchor, your heart finds its way back to Allah. Every transformation begins here — in the quiet, blessed hours of dawn, where He pours clarity, peace, and purpose upon those who rise for Him.

CHAPTER 2

The Barakah Principle:

How Allah Places Blessing Where You Show Up

There are two ways to live life:

1. By effort alone — pushing, grinding, struggling, burning out.
2. By effort *plus* barakah — where the same actions produce multiplied results, smoother outcomes, and unexpected openings.

Most Muslims today are operating in mode #1.
This book exists to shift you into mode #2.

Because barakah is not poetic.
It is not symbolic.
It is not "Islamic motivation."

Barakah is a real force.

A divine multiplier.
A spiritual catalyst that changes the nature of your time, energy, and results.

And the believer who aligns their day with Allah's design unlocks a level of clarity, strength, and productivity no secular system can match.

This chapter is about understanding that force — so the rest of the book can teach you how to *activate* it every morning.

2.1 What Is Barakah? — A Practical Definition

Most definitions of barakah are vague.

Here's the simplest way to understand it:

Barakah means: Allah puts more into something than what logic predicts.

More goodness.
More ease.
More outcomes.
More value.
More return.
More secrets.
More "how did that even happen?"

Barakah looks like:

- finishing in 1 hour what normally takes 4
- understanding in one session what others struggle with for years
- getting opportunities without chasing them
- your money stretching further than expected
- tasks flowing effortlessly
- peace settling into your home
- relationships becoming easier
- hearts becoming softer
- rizq arriving from nowhere
- ideas coming at the right time
- protection from unseen harm
- and success without the bitterness of burnout

Barakah is not "doing more."
It is being carried.

2.2 The Sunnah View of Productivity

Modern productivity says:
"Use your time efficiently."

Islam says:
"Use your time spiritually — so Allah increases what you get from it."

This is a radical difference.

The dunya teaches:

- time is limited
- output is limited
- humans must squeeze more out of less

Islam teaches:

- time expands through remembrance
- effort multiplies through sincerity
- Allah opens doors that work alone cannot
- the morning contains divine blessing
- and everything you do becomes worship with the right intention

We are not chasing "time management."
We are aligning our lives with where Allah places barakah.

That is where real transformation lies.

2.3 Why Barakah Appears in Some Lives and Not Others

Barakah is not random.
It is not luck.
It is not genetic privilege.

It follows patterns — fixed sunnah (laws) that Allah placed in the universe.

Barakah enters where five conditions meet:

1. Alignment With Allah's Commands

Barakah cannot settle into what displeases Him. It thrives where there is obedience, even if imperfect.

2. A Clean Intention

Allah multiplies what is done sincerely. Even small actions become heavy on the scale.

3. Remembrance (Dhikr)

Dhikr attracts divine presence and opens unseen doors. Anything touched by Qur'an becomes elevated.

4. Consistency

Barakah grows where actions are repeated, not rushed. What is sustained outlasts what is intense.

5. Early Mornings

The Prophet ﷺ did not simply recommend early mornings—He made du'ā specifically for this time:

> *"O Allah, bless my Ummah in their early mornings."*
>
> — *Tirmidhī*

Barakah is designed into the morning like gravity is designed into the earth.

You cannot escape it.
You can only align with it.

2.4 Why Most Muslims Don't Experience Barakah Today

The problem is not the lack of barakah. It is the lack of alignment.

We live in a time where:

- nights are wasted
- mornings are slept through
- phones dominate the first hour of the day
- stress replaces reflection
- deadlines replace dhikr
- work replaces worship
- the heart is restless
- worship feels rushed
- and life feels heavier than it should

We have adopted a lifestyle that blocks the flow of spiritual blessing, even while our souls cry out for relief.

Barakah leaves when:

- we sleep late
- we sleep after Fajr
- we neglect Qur'an
- we abandon dhikr
- we rush prayers
- we drown our minds in constant digital noise

- we rely entirely on ourselves
- we forget Allah in the first hour of the day

This book helps you reverse that drift.

2.5 The Barakah Shift: What Changes When You Live "Aligned"

When a believer aligns their life with the Qur'an, the Sunnah, and the early morning rhythm, three transformations happen:

1. The Heart Softens

Dhikr, Qur'an, and early-morning silence soften the inner world.

Anxiety reduces.
Focus returns.
You respond instead of react.
You live from the inside-out — not from panic and noise.

2. Rizq Opens

Barakah in provision is not about how many hours you work.

It is about being present in the window Allah chose for provision:
The morning.

Shaykh Samih said: *"This is the time where provisions are distributed."*

You don't have to *understand* how.
You only have to *show up*.

3. Time Expands

This is the most mysterious aspect of barakah:

Tasks take less time.
You feel less rushed.
You accomplish more with less effort.
Things flow.
Delays disappear.
Solutions appear.
People help you without you asking.

You feel *carried.*

2.6 Barakah vs Productivity: Why Muslims Need a Different Model

Every self-help guru says:

- wake up early
- avoid screens
- do deep work
- meditate
- journal
- fast
- be grateful
- contribute
- plan your day
- avoid distraction

Muslims were given something far richer:

- Fajr
- Dhikr
- Qur'an
- Du'ā
- Tawakkul
- Ṣalawāt

- Duḥā
- Early morning charity
- And a divine guarantee of barakah

The world is imitating the Sunnah without understanding its source.

We don't need to copy anyone.
We need to return to our original system.

2.7 The Morning Was Designed as a Spiritual Engine

Allah created mornings as:

- a time of clarity
- a time of purpose
- a time of angelic witness
- a time of rizq
- a time of Qur'an
- a time of remembrance
- a time of answered du'ā
- a time of productivity that is spiritually protected

This is why the Prophet ﷺ didn't simply *recommend* mornings — he ﷺ made du'ā for them, a divine request that still affects you today.

Ignoring this time is like ignoring a gift Allah placed directly in your hands.

2.8 The Core Principle of This Book

Everything you will learn in the coming chapters is built on one foundational truth:

Barakah flows where a believer meets Allah early in the day.

If you take care of this window:

- your worship deepens
- your mind sharpens
- your day stabilizes
- your heart calms
- your rizq increases
- your du'ā is uplifted
- your productivity becomes purposeful
- your dunya and ākhirah both rise

That is why all nine habits flow from the early morning. It is the spiritual root system for the rest of your life.

2.9 Why This Chapter Comes Before the Habits

Because without understanding barakah, the nine habits look like tasks. With barakah, they look like opportunities.

Without barakah, they feel heavy.
With barakah, they feel natural.

Without barakah, they are routines.
With barakah, they are transformations.

That is why we begin here. So, when you move to Chapter 3 and then into the habits, you know:

You are not just adding new practices.
You are opening the gates of divine assistance.

2.10 A Dua to Begin This Journey

Allāhumma innī as'aluka barakata fī waqtī, wa 'amalī, wa qalbī, wa rizqī, wa an taj'al ṣubḥī ibtidā'a nurin yanshuru 'alayya raḥmatak.

O Allah, I ask You for barakah in my time, my actions, my heart, and my provision. Make my morning the beginning of a light that spreads Your mercy over my life.

Āmīn.

CHAPTER 3

The Nine Habits Framework:

Your Morning Barakah System at a Glance

Before you begin the deep dive into each habit, you need a map.

This chapter gives you the entire system in one view — so you can understand:

- how all nine habits connect
- how they build on one another
- how the morning becomes a barakah engine
- how a Muslim can live with discipline and serenity
- and how to implement this system without overwhelm

This is the chapter that turns the rest of the book from "inspiring" into actionable and life changing.

3.1 What This Framework Actually Is

This is not a "routine."
It is not a "to-do list."
It is not a "perfect Muslim morning."

This is a prophetic rhythm distilled into nine simple habits:
9 Barakah Habits — designed to be done between Fajr and Duḥā

Some are verbal, some are spiritual, some are physical, some are practical.

Together, they form a complete spiritual–mental–emotional reset every single morning.

You will see this pattern over and over again.

Everything you need for a blessed life happens in the first two hours of the day.

This chapter explains *why*.

3.2 The Core Insight: These Habits Are Not Equal

Some habits anchor the system.
Some habits elevate the system.
Some habits expand the system.

To understand them properly, we categorise them into three layers:

LAYER 1 — The Anchors (Habits 1–3)

These three habits stabilise your morning. If you only did these three, your day would already transform.

Habit 1 — Stay Awake After Fajr
The foundational discipline.
It unlocks barakah, focus, clarity, and rizq.

Habit 2 — Praise and Gratitude (Al-Ḥamd)
It calibrates your mindset and opens the heart to increase, as Allah promises:

> *"If you are grateful, I will surely increase you."*
>
> — Sūrah Ibrāhīm Q14:7

Habit 3 — Tasbīḥ & Dhikr (SubḥānAllāh)
This softens the heart, clears mental noise, removes anxiety, and brings angelic presence.

Without these three habits, nothing else flows properly.
With them, everything becomes easier.

LAYER 2 — The Illuminators (Habits 4–6)

These habits *fill* your morning with light and spiritual strength.

Habit 4 — Qur'an Recitation
This is the spiritual nourishment of the day. A small portion each morning changes your entire state.

Habit 5 — Ṣalawāt on the Prophet ﷺ
A source of mercy, answered du'ā, and spiritual upliftment. One ṣalawāt brings *ten mercies* upon you.

Habit 6 — Istighfār
Repentance is the cleanser of the heart. It removes invisible blocks from your life.

> *"Seek forgiveness... He will increase you in wealth and children."*
>
> — Sūrah Nūḥ Q71:10–12

These habits cleanse, illuminate, and empower.

LAYER 3 — The Activators (Habits 7–9)

These habits move you into action with tawakkul and barakah.

Habit 7 — Duḥā Prayer
A prayer of provision, ease, contentment, and upliftment.

Habit 8 — Practical Du'ā & Tawakkul
You set your goals, tasks, and needs — and ask Allah to open the doors.
This turns your day into worship.

Habit 9 — Morning Charity & Spending
This habit attracts barakah faster than almost anything else.

> *"Charity extinguishes calamities."*
> — Jāmiʿ at-Tirmidhī

This turns your morning from spiritual intake → to spiritual output.

3.3 Why These Habits Are in This Order

This is not an arbitrary sequence.
It mirrors the structure of the soul:

1. Discipline
2. Gratitude
3. Remembrance
4. Revelation
5. Mercy
6. Cleansing
7. Worship
8. Intention
9. Giving

Each step prepares the heart for the next.

You will notice that the order moves from:

- Self-control
- Inner purification
- Connection

- Purposeful action

This is the exact way the Prophet ﷺ cultivated the sahābah.

This is the way barakah enters a life.

3.4 Why You Don't Need to Start with All Nine

Most people make this mistake: They try to do everything at once — then burn out after 4 days.

This book teaches gradual implementation:

Week 1 → Habit 1 only

Stay awake after Fajr.

Week 2 → Add Habit 2

Begin your day with praise.

Week 3 → Add Habit 3

Dhikr becomes natural.

Week 4 → Add Habit 4

Qur'an enters your morning.

And so on...

Within 9–12 weeks, you have a morning system that is:

- Consistent
- sustainable
- enjoyable
- spiritually rich

- mentally stabilising
- barakah-filled
- and aligned with your real lifestyle

This is not about pressure.
It is about transformation through ease.

3.5 Why This System Works for Every Muslim

Whether you are:

- a parent with toddlers
- a student with exams
- a corporate professional
- a shift worker
- an entrepreneur
- a stay-at-home mum
- someone struggling with stability
- someone rediscovering their faith

You can implement these habits because:
They are flexible.
They are timeless.
They are scalable.
They are Sunnah.

You do what you can with sincerity —
and Allah multiplies the impact.

3.6 The Hidden Logic Behind the Framework

This entire system is built on one spiritual truth:

You meet Allah in the morning.
Allah meets you in your day.

That is the essence of barakah.

And the nine habits are simply the *means* to this encounter.

Other systems start with willpower.
This system starts with *presence.*

Other systems start with ambition.
This system starts with *submission.*

Other systems start with the self.
This system starts with *Allah.*

This is why it works.

3.7 What You Can Expect as You Apply These Habits

Within 7–14 days:

- calmer mornings
- less stress
- more focus
- a lighter heart
- clearer thinking

Within 30 days:

- stronger īmān
- more discipline
- more emotional control
- improved sleep

- a sense of stability

Within 60–90 days:

- your whole day aligns around barakah
- your productivity becomes deep and purposeful
- your du'ā becomes more consistent
- your faith feels anchored
- you start to feel carried

Within 6 months:

- your entire life shifts
- your soul feels nourished
- your routines feel natural
- your goals feel aligned
- your relationship with Allah strengthens
- your morning becomes your sanctuary

This is the power of small prophetic habits done early, consistently, and sincerely.

3.8 What Comes Next

From here, you move into the first habit —
the one that unlocks all others:

Habit 1 — Staying Awake After Fajr

Before you build anything, you must learn how to anchor the morning.

This is where your transformation truly begins.

CHAPTER 4

Habit 1 — Staying Awake After Fajr

The Morning Awakening Blueprint

Before the sun rises, your life is already being written.
The early hours are not empty space — they are sacred architecture.
Every prophet, every saint, every scholar, every high-achieving believer anchored their life in what happens after Fajr.

And now, you are about to reclaim that window for yourself.

This habit is not about productivity.
It is about awakening — spiritually, mentally, emotionally, and physically. It is the reset that sets *everything* else in motion.

When you master the time after Fajr, you master the day.
And whoever masters the day, masters their life.

4.1 — Why the Morning Determines Your Life

There are moments in a day that shape the entire rhythm of your life. In Islam, that moment is Fajr. Not just the prayer itself, but what comes after it.

For many Muslims, the time between Fajr and sunrise goes unnoticed.
For the spiritually ambitious, this window becomes:

- a gateway to clarity
- a multiplier of barakah
- a reset for the nervous system

- a launchpad for consistency
- a hidden spiritual opportunity that the Prophet ﷺ himself prayed over

> *"O Allah, bless my ummah in their early mornings."*
> — Tirmidhī

This is not poetic language — it is a promise.
A divine endorsement of the early hours.

Modern science confirms exactly what revelation said 1,400 years ago:

- your brain is most focused within the first 2 hours after waking
- cortisol (alertness hormone) peaks after dawn
- memory retention is highest early in the morning
- the prefrontal cortex (decision-making) is sharpest
- dopamine is naturally balanced
- willpower reserves are full
- emotional regulation is strongest

When you stay awake after Fajr, you are aligning yourself with:

- biology
- fitrah
- divine barakah
- prophetic routine

That combination is unbeatable.

This habit is the first of the nine because everything else depends on it.
If you win the morning, you win the day.
If you lose the morning, the rest of the day slips through your fingers.

But here's the truth few people acknowledge:

No one wins Fajr unless they win the night.

That's why Habit 1 has two sides:

- Night Discipline → makes Fajr possible
- Morning Activation → makes the day powerful

So, before we talk about staying awake after Fajr, we must begin with the real foundation.

4.2 — Win the Night: The 3–2–1 Muslim Evening Routine

The night is preparation. The morning is execution.
You cannot build a powerful morning on a weak night.

Even the most spiritually ambitious believer will collapse if they:

- stay up pointlessly
- overstimulate their mind
- eat heavy late at night
- enter sleep in a state of heedlessness

A blessed morning begins hours before Fajr — with the way you unwind, the way you silence the noise of the day, and the way you hand your night to Allah.

This is your **evening blueprint** to:

- calm your nervous system
- reset your heart
- protect your sleep
- end your day with Allah
- prepare your soul for the barakah of Fajr

The 3–2–1 System

A Modern Framework Rooted in Prophetic Sleep Principles

The **3–2–1 system** is a simple rule for preparing your mind and body for deep, restorative sleep. The numbers are modern; the wisdom is Prophetic.

The Prophet ﷺ:

- slept early
- avoided pointless late-night talk
- kept his stomach light in the evening
- recited dhikr before sleeping
- forgave others
- maintained emotional calm at night

This is exactly what psychology and neuroscience now call "optimal sleep hygiene."

3 Hours Before Sleep → No Food

Late-night eating forces the body into biological conflict. Instead of resting, your body must:

- digest while you sleep
- raise internal temperature
- reduce deep sleep and REM cycles
- increase morning fogginess
- spike cortisol and stress levels

The Prophet ﷺ rarely ate late — not only as spiritual discipline, but as profound physiological wisdom.

Light evening. Light stomach. Clear Fajr.

2 Hours Before Sleep → No Drinking

Not strict fiqh — practical mercy.

Reducing liquids before sleep means:

- fewer bathroom disruptions
- deeper, more stable sleep cycles
- less midnight agitation
- calmer waking

If you struggle with fragmented sleep, this one change can be life changing.

The goal is simple: give your body a peaceful descent into rest.

1 Hour Before Sleep → No Screens

This is the real game-changer.

Blue light and late-night stimulation:

- suppress melatonin (your sleep hormone)
- over-activate your brain
- trick your mind into "daytime mode"
- disrupt circadian rhythm
- increase anxiety and emotional reactivity

You **cannot** overstimulate your brain with scrolling and expect to wake up spiritually alive.

Replace screens with:

- Qur'ān
- dhikr
- soft, calming reading
- light journaling

- silence and dim lighting
- light stretching / deep breathing
- mindful stillness

These activities signal to your brain that the day is ending — and that your heart is returning to Allah.

Let the nervous system soften.
Let the mind land.
Let the night become a bridge to barakah.

The Shutdown Ritual (10–20 Minutes)

The 3–2–1 system sets the boundaries of your night.
The Shutdown Ritual closes your day with intention.

Think of it as your nightly "log-off" — Islamic, simple, and repeatable.

1. Shutdown for the Day — *The 5-Minute Barakah Planner*

A powerful morning begins the night before.
Set the stage for ease, clarity, and obedience. These simple steps remove friction and make it *natural* to meet the dawn with purpose.

Clear the space around you — *2 minutes*

- put items away
- switch off harsh lights
- tidy key surfaces
- close obvious "open loops" e.g. laptop, scattered notes

A clean environment unclutters the heart and tells your brain: "*We are done for today.*"

Sit for a minute and acknowledge quietly — *2–3 minutes*

- what today took from you
- what you received today
- where you handled things well
- where you slipped

Then say:

"Yā Allah, I hand this day back to You."

You're not replaying everything — you're releasing it.
Sleep becomes healing instead of heavy.

2. Set Your Intention Before You Sleep

Before you fall asleep, remind yourself of your purpose:
you want to meet Fajr with strength, presence, and sincerity.

Speak to Allah from your heart — not as a replacement for the Sunnah adhkār of the night, but as an *addition* to them.

After completing the **authentic du'ā's and adhkār prescribed for bedtime**, take a moment to make your personal intention. Something simple and sincere, such as: *"Yā Allah, help me rise for Fajr with clarity, energy, and sincerity."*

This is not a formal prophetic du'ā'.
It is your own niyyah — your personal conversation with Allah.

A sincere intention before sleep reshapes *how* you sleep, *why* you wake, and *what your heart is aiming for* at dawn. It gently trains your mind and soul to honour those early hours.

3. Qur'an Wind-Down & Sunnah Sleep Adab

Night Dua — *4–6 minutes*

- Āyat al-Kursī
- the last two āyat of Sūrat al-Baqarah
- Sūrat al-Ikhlāṣ, al-Falaq and al-Nās (3× each)
- dhikr of closure:
  - SubḥānAllāh (33×)
  - Alḥamdulillāh (33×)
  - Allāhu Akbar (34×)

Then say the sleep du'ā':

بِاسْمِكَ رَبِّ وَضَعْتُ جَنْبِي،وَبِكَ أَرْفَعُهُ، إِنْ أَمْسَكْتَ نَفْسِي فَاغْفِرْ لَهَا،
وَإِنْ أَرْسَلْتَهَا فَاحْفَظْهَا بِمَا تَحْفَظُ بِهِ عِبَادَكَ الصَّالِحِينَ

"Bismika rabbī waḍa'tu janbī wabika arfa'uhu. In amsakta nafsī faghfir lahā, wa in arsaltahā faḥfaẓhā bimā taḥfaẓ bihī 'ibādaka aṣ-ṣāliḥīn."

In Your name, my Lord, I lay my side down, and by You I lift it up. If You take my soul, forgive it. If You return it, protect it just as You protect Your righteous servants.

"Allāhumma bismika amūtu wa aḥyā."

"O Allah, solely in Your Name I die and I live."

Choose ONE for *3–5 minutes:*

- Sūrah al-Mulk
- Sūrah as-Sajdah
- 1–2 pages of Qur'an
- gentle, audio recitation

Then sleep with the Sunnah adab:

- sleep on your right side first
- place your hand under your cheek
- avoid sleeping on your stomach
- keep the environment dim and as quiet as reasonably possible
- sleep as early as you can after 'Ishā'

These are not symbolic.
They are shields. Spiritual force fields. Protection while you sleep.

4. Clearing the Heart Before Sleep

Before you close your eyes, release the weight of the day.

The Prophet ﷺ taught that forgiveness is a gateway to Allah's mercy and that those who hold hatred between them can be blocked from forgiveness.

For your heart to stay light, you must sleep with:

- no grudges
- no revenge plans
- no bitterness
- no poison

He taught that a believer who sleeps with a clean heart — free of hatred and bitterness — is among the best of people. One companion was described by the Prophet ﷺ as a "man of Paradise," and when asked why, he revealed only this:

"I do not sleep except that my heart is free of ill will towards any Muslim."

Let the night be your emotional reset.
Grant forgiveness, even silently.

Let go of what bruised you.
Free your heart from carrying what Allah never asked you to hold.

Forgiving others doesn't make you weak;
it makes your *du'ā'* get answered and your sleep lighter.

Carry *no emotional burden* into the night — so you can rise for Fajr with a heart that is open, soft, and ready for barakah

Say before sleep (in your own language if needed):

> *"Yā Allah, I forgive everyone who wronged me today.*
> *Forgive me as I forgive them."*

You sleep with mercy — you wake with barakah.

These steps are not "self-help hacks."
They are **Sunnah-backed psychology**—actions that align your environment with your intentions, creating a path of least resistance toward obedience.

The Prophet ﷺ taught us to *prepare* for worship, to *remove obstacles*, and to *choose ease* where Allah allowed ease.

This is simply that wisdom applied to your morning.

When you prepare the night before, you're telling your soul:

"Tomorrow matters."

Good sleep → good Fajr.
Good Fajr → good day.

The Night Routine Summary (Quick Check Card)

- No food after ______________
- No water after ______________
- Screens off at ______________
- Pray 'Ishā' with presence ☐
- Qur'ān recitation ☐
- 3 Quls + Ayat al-Kursī ☐
- Du'ā' for the morning ☐
- Prepare clothing/workspace ☐
- Sleep with the intention of worship ☐
- Release your heart so it can rest light and clean ☐

This is how believers sleep with strategy, not accident.

4.3 — Why Not Sleeping After Fajr Multiplies Blessings

If you hold onto this one habit,
you will start to see blessings everywhere.

Why?

Because Allah places the day's *rizq*, *creativity*, and *productivity* in the early hours.

- The ummah's barakah lives in early morning
- Provisions are distributed after Fajr
- Minds are sharpest
- Hearts are calmest
- Angels witness this time
- Intentions are renewed
- Energy multiplies

Sleeping after Fajr is allowed, but you lose the barakah window.

Remaining awake after Fajr leads to:

- clarity
- focus
- purposeful action
- deeper iman
- consistency
- better time management
- emotional resilience
- mental sharpness
- increased rizq (spiritually and materially)

It is the first domino that knocks down the rest of your day in the right direction.

4.4 — What Should You Actually DO After Fajr?

A practical, guided sequence.

This is the Morning Awakening Blueprint:

1. Pray Fajr on time
2. Stay awake (10–120 min based on level)
3. Step outside or open a window
4. Morning adhkār
5. Qur'ān recitation / memorisation
6. Ṣalawāt
7. Du'ā'
8. Deep work or intentional movement
9. Duḥā prayer (2–8 rak'ah)

Even *10 minutes* after Fajr done consciously is transformative.

4.5 — Real-Life Muslim Morning Routines

The Corporate & Working Professional

A professional's morning is shaped by deadlines, emails, meetings, commuting, and the constant pressure of performance.
But with intention and structure, it becomes a **barakah engine** — a source of clarity, strength, and excellence that affects the entire workday.

This routine is designed for **real life**, not ideal circumstances.

1. Fajr

Pray with calm.
Don't rush into dunya.
Let your heart arrive before your body moves.

2. Sit 5–10 Minutes After Fajr —*Spiritual Activation Window*

This pocket is your anchor.

Read or recite:

- Ayatul Kursi
- 3 Quls
- selected morning adhkār
- a short du'ā' for barakah, ease, and success

This **tiny sitting** protects you from stress, decision fatigue, and emotional heaviness in the office.

3. Qur'ān (½ page → 1 page)

High-impact, low-pressure reading.

Choose ONE:

- reading
- memorisation
- reflection (tafakkur)

Professionals rarely have long stretches of calm — this small dose sets your entire day on a higher spiritual frequency.

4. Shower + Get Ready — *Mind Reset Phase*

This is more than grooming — it's psychological reset.

- alertness increases
- intention recalibrates
- confidence rises
- presence returns

A clean, intentional start influences how you carry yourself at work.

5. Support the Home — *If Applicable*

Many professionals begin the day with family and responsibilities.

Keep this phase simple:

- help prepare breakfast
- support kids getting ready
- assist spouse/parents where needed
- quick household touch-ups

Even minor acts of service invite enormous barakah into your workday.

6. Breakfast

A stable meal = a stable professional.

Avoid heavy foods that crash your energy.
Prioritise light, sustaining choices.

7. Commute — The Professional's Untapped Barakah Window

This is the *secret advantage* professionals waste.

On your walk, drive, bus, or train:

- complete remaining morning adhkār
- and/or listen to Qur'an
- and/or listen to a 5–10 minute Islamic reminder
- and/or make quiet du'ā' for your tasks, meetings, and decisions
- and/or mentally organise your top 3 priorities

This transforms "lost time" into spiritual and mental alignment.

While colleagues scroll or complain, you ascend.

8. Arrive Early for Your Barakah Hour (If Possible)

If your role allows it, arriving **10–20 minutes before the office wakes up** is a game-changer.

Use this quiet pocket for:

- deep work
- strategic thinking
- clearing critical tasks
- preparing for key meetings
- reviewing documents

This calm window produces more clarity and output than the next three reactive hours combined.

If arriving early is not possible, use the first minutes at your desk to:

- take a breath
- set intention
- write the day's top 3 tasks
- quietly say "Bismillāh" before beginning

Why This Routine Works for Professionals

It balances:

✔ Spiritual grounding
Without overwhelming your morning.

✔ Real home responsibilities
Family, preparation, and life admin are acknowledged, not ignored.

✔ Cognitive science
The brain is sharpest in the early morning — perfect for Qur'an + clarity tasks.

✔ Commute optimisation
This is the biggest untapped barakah window for working adults.

✔ Workplace performance alignment
This routine makes you calmer, clearer, more disciplined, more intentional — and noticeably better at your job.

It's realistic.
It's achievable.
It's transformative.

The Student

A smart, barakah-aligned student **doesn't waste the golden morning window** on what could have been done the night before.

The *best hour for understanding* — post-Fajr to sunrise — should NEVER be used for tidying, packing, hunting for books, or rushing.

That hour belongs to:

- Qur'an
- Dhikr
- Reflection
- the highest-value academic work (light review, deep understanding, memorisation)

The Night Before —Foundational Step

A wise student prepares so they don't waste the barakah window.

- pack school/uni bag
- lay out uniform or clothes
- charge devices
- tidy room for 1–2 minutes
- glance at tomorrow's timetable
- prepare lunch/snacks
- set intention for the morning

This turns the next morning into FLOW rather than FRICTION.

The Morning Routine

1. Fajr
Pray with presence.
Begin the day anchored, not rushed.

2. Sit 5–10 Minutes After Fajr — *Spiritual Activation Window*

This is the most accessible and powerful student habit.

Recite:

- Ayatul Kursi
- the 3 Quls
- core morning adhkār
- a short duʿāʾ for success, ease, and protection

This small sitting stabilises the heart for the entire school day.

3. Qur'ān — *½ – 1 page*

Choose ONE:

- reading
- memorisation
- tafsir reflection

Consistency is more important than quantity.
Even **half a page** daily can transform the mind and memory over a year.

4. Sunrise Academic Review — *The Best Hour for Understanding*

This is **gold** for students.

NOT heavy studying —
but a light revision of:

- yesterday's notes
- key definitions
- formulas
- summaries
- lecture highlights

The brain is chemically primed at this hour to absorb and understand fast. What you revise here will stay with you all day.

This one habit separates high-achieving students from average ones.

5. Get Ready — *Smooth + Fast*

Because everything was prepared the night before, there is:

- no rushing
- no searching for books
- no last-minute chaos

Just:

- bathing
- dressing
- simple grooming
- a calm transition into the day

A peaceful student is a sharp student.

6. Breakfast

A simple, stable meal.
Blood sugar affects concentration more than motivation does.

7. Commute — The Hidden Barakah Window

This is where students finish their morning adhkār.

During the walk/bus/train ride:

- complete morning adhkār
- review memorisation
- listen to Qur'an
- make du'ā' for the day
- mentally preview responsibilities

For students, **this is one of the best spiritual pockets of the day** because the body is moving but the mind is free.

8. Arrive 10–20 Minutes Early

This is an academic superpower.

Use this quiet time for:

- a brief reading
- organising materials
- finalising memorisation
- pre-learning (glancing at today's topics)
- calming your mind before classes begin

This short pocket builds confidence and removes anxiety for the whole day.

The Stay-at-Home Mother

A Gentle, Realistic, Barakah-Optimised Routine

A mother's morning is rarely quiet.
It is shaped by night wakings, feeding schedules, school runs, household responsibilities, and the constant emotional labour of nurturing a family.

Yet with intention and small, strategic habits, your morning can become one of the **most spiritually powerful and emotionally stabilising** parts of your day — even when life feels chaotic.

This routine honours your reality, not an idealised version of it.

The Night Before — Your Lifeline

When possible, a few minutes the night before can transform the next morning:

- prep school uniforms
- pack bags
- set aside outfits for younger children
- tidy the living area for 1–2 minutes
- Place Qur'an or dhikr book somewhere accessible
- prepare breakfast ingredients (even small steps)
- set an intention for the following morning

None of this has to be perfect — *even tiny preparation reduces morning overwhelm.*

The Morning Routine

Flexible + Gentle + Spiritually Grounded

1. Fajr

Pray as soon as possible, even if the night was difficult.
If the baby needs you immediately afterward, you are rewarded for that too.

A mother's Fajr is often the most heroic act of the day.

2. Sit for 3–5 Minutes After Fajr
The Calm-Heart Window

Mothers rarely get long pockets of silence — so keep this short, achievable, and powerful.

Use these few minutes for:

- Ayatul Kursi
- the 3 Quls
- 1–2 core morning adhkār
- a short du'ā' for patience, ease, and barakah

This small pause becomes your emotional anchor for the entire day.

3. Qur'ān (Micro-Portion: 2–5 minutes)

For many mothers:

- ½ page
- a few āyat
- a single reflection
- listening while feeding or prepping

...is more realistic and more sustainable than traditional study sessions.

Consistency here is what brings barakah, not quantity.

4. Children Wake / Household Duties Begin

This phase varies daily — and that's okay.

It may involve:

- feeding the baby
- preparing breakfast
- dressing children
- supporting school readiness
- helping with emotional regulation
- calming morning chaos

Every act of service **counts as ibādah** when done with intention.

5. Serve With Dhikr —The Mother's Secret Barakah Habit

Instead of trying to "find time," **layers dhikr into what you are already doing**:

- "Bismillah" while dressing children
- "Alhamdulillah" while preparing meals
- "SubḥānAllāh" while tidying
- Salawāt while packing lunches
- Quiet du'ā' while soothing a child

This turns motherhood into a continuous act of worship — effortless and deeply rewarded.

6. Breakfast — *Your's + the Family's*

A simple, calm breakfast helps stabilise:

- patience
- mood
- energy
- emotional resilience

A mother's nutrition is not a luxury — it's fuel for her day.

7. School Run / Morning Movement

The walk or drive becomes a **barakah window**:

- completing morning adhkār
- listening to Qur'an
- salawāt
- making du'ā' for your children
- reflecting on your intentions

This is often the only uninterrupted spiritual time you get — turn it into a blessing, not wasted minutes.

8. Home Reset — 5–10 Minutes Only

Once back home (or after breakfast if children are still home), do a **tiny reset**:

- clear one surface
- start one load of laundry
- open windows for light and airflow

This prevents overwhelm and creates emotional clarity.

Not cleaning the whole house — just *resetting her environment* so she feels in control, not consumed.

Why This Routine Works for Mothers

✔ It's flexible
No guilt if the baby cried, if Fajr was hard, or the morning exploded.
✔ It's micro-based
Tiny spiritual actions that carry big weight.
✔ It respects emotional labour
Mothers carry more than tasks — they carry hearts.
✔ It integrates worship into daily life
She doesn't "lose out" when busy; she accumulates reward.
✔ It stabilises her mental and emotional state
A regulated mother is a more patient mother.
✔ It produces real barakah
Her home becomes peaceful, her heart becomes lighter, and her day becomes easier.

The Busy Mother

A High-Demand, High-Barakah Morning Framework

The busy mother carries multiple roles at once: professional, caregiver, homemaker, emotional anchor, and often the unseen manager of the entire household.

Her mornings are fast, layered, and often unpredictable.

This routine is built to **reduce overwhelm**, **increase barakah**, and give her a structure she can maintain — even on the hardest days.

The Night Before — The Busy Mother's Lifeline

The most impactful minute of the whole morning is actually the one spent the night before.

Prepare:

- clothes for work
- children's clothes
- bags (school + work)
- quick tidy of shared spaces
- breakfast prep (even small steps matter)
- set tomorrow's top 3 priorities
- place Qur'an / adhkār book where you will see

She doesn't need a perfect home —
she needs a **friction-free morning**.

The Morning Routine

Flexible, Grounded, Short, Powerful

1. Fajr

A mother's Fajr is heroic.
No matter how tired, she shows up.

Pray, breathe, and give yourself permission not to rush into the next task.

2. 3–5 Minutes of Spiritual Anchoring

Because she operates under time pressure, her spiritual core needs to be short but strong.

In this window:

- Ayatul Kursi
- the 3 Quls
- 1–2 morning adhkār
- a short du'ā' for ease, patience, and barakah

This small grounding dramatically shifts her emotional state.

3. Qur'ān (Micro Portion: 2–5 mins)

A busy mother doesn't need long sessions — she needs **consistency**.

Choose:

- ½ page
- a few ayāt
- listening while getting ready
- one reflection āyat

This keeps you connected and spiritually nourished before the day intensifies.

4. Morning Flow (Family + House + Self)

This phase is layered and multitasking-heavy.

It may include:

- waking children
- preparing breakfast
- packing lunches
- ironing uniforms
- managing emotions and morning resistance
- getting yourself ready for work
- feeding babies or toddlers
- coordinating with spouse or family support

This is not "chaos" — this is **service done with intention**.

Your dhikr during this time carries immeasurable reward.

5. Serve With Dhikr — *Barakah Multiplier*

Layered dhikr into tasks:

- "Bismillāh" while preparing meals
- "SubhānAllāh" while tidying
- "Alḥamdulillāh" while dressing children
- Salawāt while driving or waiting

This transforms mundane tasks into worship and reduces internal pressure.

6. Breakfast — Yours + the Family's

Many busy mothers forget themselves.

A small, balanced breakfast improves:

- patience
- mood

- mental clarity
- decision-making
- energy levels

She cannot pour from an empty tank.

7. Commute — Her Hidden Barakah Window

This is often the ONLY silence she gets.

Use it for:

- completing adhkār
- listening to Qur'an
- making du'ā' for work, home, children
- mentally organising her day
- deep breathing and emotional grounding

This transforms the commute from stress to serenity.

8. Arrival at Work / School Run Completion

Before diving into her responsibilities:

Take **30 seconds**.
Breathe.
Set intention.
Say: "Bismillāh, Yā Allah make this day easy and accepted."

This micro-transition shifts her from reactive to focused.

Why This Routine Works for Busy Mothers

✓ It's flexible — not rigid
Works on the best days and the worst days.

✓ It is realistic — no unrealistic time blocks
Just tiny, powerful micro-habits.
✓ It integrates worship into daily tasks
No need to carve out missing hours.
✓ It addresses emotional load
Busy mothers need spiritual calm, not more tasks.
✓ It honours her sacrifices
Every action becomes reward when paired with the right intention.
✓ It leads to higher patience + mental clarity
She starts the day spiritually fed, not depleted.

The Single Mother

A Strength-Based, Barakah-Driven Morning System

A single mother carries a weight most people will never see:
the responsibilities of two people, the emotional labour of a household, the financial concerns, the schedule management, the decision-making — all while striving to stay spiritually anchored.

Her mornings require gentleness, strategy, and barakah.
This routine is designed to **support her, not overwhelm her** — to give her a structure that strengthens rather than drains.

The Night Before

The Single Mother's Protection Against Morning Overwhelm

Even small preparation the night before dramatically reduces morning stress.

Priorities:

- school bags packed
- clothes laid out (hers + the children's)

- quick tidy of living area (1–2 minutes only)
- note down tomorrow's top 3 tasks
- prep easy breakfast items
- place Qur'an in a visible, reachable spot

This allows her to enter the morning with **clarity, not chaos.**

The Morning Routine

Strong, Gentle, Achievable

1. **Fajr**

Show up for Allah even with a tired heart.
This moment is your lifeline — a reminder that you are never alone in your struggles.

Fajr for a single mother is not small;
it is an act of courage.

2. **3–7 Minutes of Spiritual Grounding**

Short, powerful, and mentally calming.

Recite:

- Ayatul Kursi
- 3 Quls
- a few core morning adhkār
- a duʿāʾ for strength, patience, and rizq

This grounding stabilises emotional turbulence and sets the tone for the day.

3. **Qur'ān — Micro Portion**

Realistic, compassionate expectations:

- ½ page
- a few ayāt
- listening while dressing
- reflection on one āyah

Consistency here **protects her heart** and replenishes what life drains.

4. Morning Flow — Children + Household Tasks

This period is often your busiest:

- waking and dressing children
- breakfast preparation
- packing bags
- calming emotional moments
- managing school readiness
- getting yourself ready for the day

She carries multiple roles at once.
Every act, with the right intention, becomes ibādah.

5. Dhikr Layered into Tasks - *Your Barakah Multiplier*

One of the most powerful habits you can build is **integrating dhikr into the tasks you already do**.
You don't need long sessions.
You don't need silence.
You don't need extra time.

Just begin every task with: *"Bismillāh."*

That one word turns your entire morning into worship.

Everything that follows is simply a suggestion — you may choose any dhikr you love.

While preparing food:
Repeat: *"Alḥamdulillāh."*
Let gratitude flow into the meal you're creating.
This simple remembrance invites more provision, more ease, and more contentment into your home.

While planning finances or feeling the weight of responsibility:
Recite the du'ā' the Prophet ﷺ taught:

"Allāhumma ighfir lī dhambī, wa wassi' lī fī dārī, wa bārik lī fī rizqī."

"O Allah, forgive my sins, expand my home, and bless my provision."

And whisper: *"Yā Razzaq urzuqni."*
"O Provider, provide for me".

He is the One who provides — sometimes from places you never imagined.

While tidying or resetting the home:
Repeat:
"SubḥānAllāh, wal-ḥamdu lillāh, wa lā ilāha illAllāh, wallāhu Akbar."

"Glory be to Allah, and praise be to Allah, and there is no god but Allah, and Allah is the Greatest."

As your space becomes lighter, so does your heart.

During quiet moments or small pauses:
Send **ṣalawāt** upon the Prophet ﷺ.
Allāhumma ṣalli 'alā Muḥammad wa 'alā āli Muḥammad.

"O Allah, honour and have mercy upon Muhammad and his household."

It brings peace to your chest and puts blessings into your day.

When the morning feels heavy or overwhelming:
Say: *"Yā Allah, make it easy."*

A short du'ā' with a long reach.

Your Principle of the Morning:
You don't need extra hours.
You don't need a perfect environment.
You don't need silence or structure.

*You simply need **remembrance woven into movement**.*

As you prepare, clean, walk, carry, organise, or settle your children, your dhikr becomes the soundtrack of your morning.

It nourishes your heart.
It protects your mind.
It strengthens your spirit.
And it brings barakah into every corner of your day.

6. Breakfast — *Yours + Your Children's*

You cannot pour into anyone if you are running on empty — not emotionally, not mentally, and not physically.

A simple, steady breakfast does more for you than most people realise.
It helps regulate your:

- mood
- stress levels
- mental clarity
- physical energy

And here's the truth you often forget:

You deserve nourishment too.

Not just the leftovers, not a rushed bite, not whatever is convenient. You deserve food that supports your body, stabilises your day, and honours the effort you give to your family and yourself.

Even something small and simple — eaten with intention — becomes fuel, barakah, and care for your own wellbeing.

7. Commute / School Run — *Your Emotional Reset Window*

This might be the only uninterrupted moment you get all morning. Instead of letting it become a time of tension or rush, turn it into your **reset window**.

Use this time to:

- complete your morning adhkār
- listen to Qur'an
- play an uplifting reminder
- make du'ā' for yourself and your children
- take slow, grounding breaths to regulate your nervous system

In these small pockets of stillness — while walking, driving, or sitting on a bus — you reconnect to yourself and to Allah.

This is how your commute transforms from pressure into peace,
from stress into serenity,
from noise into nourishment.

8. Arrival (Home or Work) — *Your 30-Second Reset*

Before you dive into the next wave of responsibilities, give yourself half a minute to pause.

Just:

- take one deep breath
- set a quiet intention
- and say:
  "Yā Allah, I leave today in Your hands."

This simple transition shifts you from **surviving the day** to **walking through it with Allah beside you**.

It stabilises your emotions, clears your mind, and reminds you that you are never carrying this life alone.

Why This Routine Works for Single Mothers

✓ It respects her capacity
No unrealistic blocks. Just powerful micro-habits.
✓ It acknowledges her emotional labour
The routine stabilises her internally, not just spiritually.
✓ It integrates worship into her reality
She doesn't "lose out" when busy — she gains barakah through intention.
✓ It prevents morning overwhelm
Night-before prep + a structured flow = calmer mornings.
✓ It builds spiritual resilience
Makes her feel supported, grounded, and strengthened.
✓ It turns her morning into a source of emotional healing
Her heart is fed before the world demands from her.

The Entrepreneur

A Clarity-Driven, Barakah-Focused Morning Routine

Your mornings shape your momentum.
When you run a business — whether from home, an office, a laptop, or your phone — you need a routine that gives you clarity, direction, and barakah before the demands of clients, customers, and creativity pull you into the day.

This is your morning system — simple, powerful, and built for long-term stability.

The Night Before

Your Entrepreneurial Advantage

Your next day becomes 10× easier when you prepare the night before.

Do this in 5 -10 minutes:

- write tomorrow's top 3 priorities
- review your calendar
- pre-decide what "success" looks like for the day
- tidy your workspace for 1–2 minutes
- place your Qur'an or dhikr book on your desk
- shut down fully — entrepreneurs rarely rest properly

This primes your brain to enter the morning with clarity instead of chaos.

The Morning Routine

Barakah First, Business Second

1. Fajr

Your entire entrepreneurial mindset resets here.
Pray, breathe, and begin the day with the One who controls all outcomes.

2. Sit 5–10 Minutes After Fajr

The Entrepreneur's Strategic Stillness

Use this quiet window to recite:

- Ayatul Kursi
- the 3 Quls
- a few core morning adhkār
- a short du'ā' for guidance, creativity, focus, and barakah in your work

This grounding protects you from overwhelm and decision fatigue later.

3. Qur'ān (½ page → 1 page)

A small portion of Qur'an sharpens your mind, softens your heart, and increases clarity.

Choose:

- memorisation
- reading
- reflection

Your best ideas often come **after Qur'an**, not before.

4. Get Ready — *Reset Your State*

Shower, dress with intention, and present yourself as the CEO of your day.
Your physiology affects your psychology.

A refreshed state sharpens:

- confidence
- presence
- creativity

- decision-making

5. Morning Home Duties ***(If Applicable)***

If you're caring for children or supporting family, integrate dhikr into everything you do.

Say *"Bismillāh"* before each task and choose any dhikr that flows naturally into movement.

Your service at home carries barakah into your business.

6. Breakfast

Entrepreneurs burn mental energy fast.
A simple, stable breakfast fuels focus, mood, and stamina.

This is not indulgence — it's strategy.

7. Commute / Transition to Work — ***Your Alignment Window***

Whether you're walking to your office, driving, or simply moving from your bedroom to your desk:

Use this window for:

- completing adhkār
- listening to Qur'an
- setting your intention
- visualising your top 3 outcomes
- making du'ā' for clarity, openings, and ease

This moment aligns your heart before your business pulls you in.

8. Begin With Your Barakah Hour

Deep Work Before the World Wakes Up

Your **first hour of work** determines your entire day.

Use it for:

- strategy
- creativity
- writing
- planning
- problem-solving
- building, not reacting

No emails.
No messages.
No task-switching.
No scrolling.

This is the hour where Allah multiplies your outcomes.

One barakah-filled hour in the morning equals
three reactive hours in the afternoon.

Why This Routine Works for Entrepreneurs

✔ It protects your mental bandwidth
You start grounded, not scattered.

✔ It prioritises deep work
Entrepreneurs live and die by focus.

✔ It aligns your work with Allah
This Reduces Fear, Stress, and Uncertainty.

✔ It uses science + spirituality
Morning clarity + barakah = unstoppable momentum.

✔ It is adaptable

Whether you're running a full business, freelancing, or working from home, this routine fits your rhythm.

4.6 — Your 30-Day Stay-Awake-After-Fajr Plan

Week 1 — Awareness

Your First Step Toward a Barakah Morning

The goal of Week 1 is not perfection — it is *awareness.*
You're training your body and mind to stop collapsing back into bed after Fajr. This week is about *small wins* that build identity, not intensity.

Stay awake for 5–10 minutes
Right after Fajr, resist the urge to lie down "just for a moment."
Stand, stretch, walk to the kitchen — anything that keeps you alert.
These first 10 minutes are your anchor.

Sit with tea or water
Create a calming ritual: warm tea, a glass of water, or a light herbal drink. This helps signal to your brain that the day has begun and reduces the pull of sleep.

Do minimal dhikr
Keep it simple and sustainable:

- SubḥānAllāh (33×)
- Alḥamdulillāh (33×)
- Allāhu Akbar (34×) or
- Morning "lā ilāha illa Allāh" in any number.

This is not about quantity — it's about presence.
You're teaching your heart to *associate wakefulness with remembrance.*

The purpose of Week 1:

- Become conscious of your post-Fajr behaviour
- Break the automatic habit of returning to sleep
- Build a gentle, enjoyable morning experience
- Prove to yourself: "I can stay awake for a short period"

Week 1 is the psychological breakthrough.
Once your body learns, "We don't sleep after Fajr," the next weeks become far easier.

Week 2 — Activation

Build Momentum with Intention and Light Action

Week 1 taught your body to *stay awake.*
Now Week 2 teaches it to *activate.*

You're not just awake — you're stepping into a purposeful morning.

Increase to 15–25 minutes
Extend your wakefulness window.
This is long enough to energise the body yet short enough to stay sustainable.

If 25 feels too far, aim for 20.
If 20 feels too far, aim for 15.
Growth is the win — not perfection.

Add Qur'ān
Introduce a short, manageable recitation routine:

- Half a page
- One page
- Or even five āyat

Choose consistency over ambition.
You're teaching your heart that the first light of your day belongs to Allah.

This single habit alone transforms the emotional tone of your morning.

Morning fresh air

Step outside to your doorstep, balcony, garden, or open a window wide. Fresh air + early sunlight does three things:

- signals "morning mode" to the brain
- increases alertness and serotonin
- boosts your overall mood

This small step dramatically reduces sleepiness and stabilises your circadian rhythm.

The purpose of Week 2:

- Activate your mind and senses
- Introduce gentle worship into your morning window
- Strengthen the identity of "I am someone who stays awake after Fajr"
- Build the biological foundation for long-term consistency

By the end of Week 2, you won't just be awake —
you'll be *moving*, *breathing*, and *reciting*.

You will feel the shift.

Week 3 — Discipline

Multiply Your Morning Barakah with Purposeful Habits

By Week 3, something beautiful happens:
Your body *expects* to stay awake after Fajr, and your heart begins to feel the calm of early-morning presence.

Now it's time to **expand** — gently, intentionally, and sustainably.

You're not adding pressure.
You're adding *purpose.*

Stay awake for 30–45 minutes
This extended window becomes your personal sanctuary.
Long enough to create flow, short enough to avoid overwhelm.

Even 30 consistent minutes in the early morning can outperform hours of scattered effort later in the day.

Add reflective reading or journaling
Choose one:

- A page from a beneficial Islamic book
- A reflection from a tafsīr
- A short journaling prompt ("What is one intention I will carry today?")

This builds *spiritual clarity* and reduces the mental clutter that usually arrives mid-morning.

Your goal here is alignment, not productivity.

Introduce a light physical movement
Gentle stretching, a short walk, or mobility work.
This:

- increases alertness

- stabilises mood
- improves energy
- strengthens consistency

You're teaching your body that morning equals movement, not grogginess.

Optional: Begin a micro-goal
A small, barakah-aligned habit such as:

- 5 minutes of language learning
- Reviewing two flashcards
- Planning top 3 priorities of the day

Micro-goals build identity:
"I use my mornings for growth."

The purpose of Week 3:

- Deepen your presence after Fajr
- Layer small, meaningful habits without burnout
- Create an environment where staying awake feels natural
- Strengthen emotional stability and focus at the start of the day
- Connect your spiritual rhythm with practical living

By the end of Week 3, your mornings are no longer an obligation — they're becoming a lifestyle.

Week 4 — Mastery

Turn Your After-Fajr Routine into a Permanent Way of Life

By Week 4, something subtle but profound has shifted:
You're no longer "trying" to stay awake after Fajr —
you're *becoming a person who does.*

Now the goal of this final week is **consolidation**.
You're stabilising everything you've built so that this routine becomes part of who you are, not something you fight for.

This is where barakah becomes a rhythm.

Stay awake for 45–60+ minutes
This is the full expression of your morning.
Long enough to:

- recite Qur'ān with calm
- think clearly
- begin meaningful work
- align your entire day with purpose

You're not chasing a number — you're claiming your morning.

Lock in your Qur'ān routine

Choose one permanent practice:

- One page daily
- A set number of āyat
- A short study + reflection
- Revision of memorised surahs

This becomes the *core* of your barakah morning.
A habit that anchors your heart and mind, even during busy seasons.

Add intentional planning for the day

Spend 3–5 minutes answering:

- What matters most today?
- What can wait?

- What will I do with excellence for Allah's sake?

Planning in the after-Fajr window carries a different kind of clarity — It is free from noise, ego, and external pressure.

Optional: Begin your first major "Barakah Project"

You may now have the stability to start something meaningful:

- memorising a surah
- learning Arabic
- launching a small habit
- building a consistent exercise routine
- starting a journal of duʿāʾ and gratitude

If it feels too heavy, leave it.
Mastery is consistency, not overload.

Build your "Master Morning Environment"

Make small adjustments that lock the identity in:

- keep a designated Qur'ān spot
- place your notebook and pen nearby
- keep a water bottle ready
- maintain a quiet environment between Fajr and sunrise

Consistency comes from the environment more than motivation.

The purpose of Week 4:

- Transition out of "I am trying" → into "This is who I am"
- Stabilise the habits built over the first three weeks
- Create a dependable, spiritually rooted morning rhythm
- Strengthen the emotional and mental clarity of your early hours
- Build a permanent connection between Fajr and purpose

By the end of Week 4, you will have built a system — not a streak.
A way of life — not a challenge.
A new identity — not another "self-help routine."

4.7 — When You Struggle or Miss a Day

Even with the best intentions, there will be mornings that feel heavy, rushed, or simply off. This is normal. What matters is how you recover — not whether you stumbled.

If You Feel Burnout

When your body or heart feels drained:

- **Simplify your morning** —Reduce your morning to the essentials: Fajr, one dhikr, one breath of fresh air.
- **Fix the night before you push the morning** — Use the Minimum Night Routine instead of forcing a heroic after-Fajr streak.
- **Lower your expectations** — Not every day will feel powerful. Consistency is built on gentleness.
- **Return to the Beginner Routine** — Sometimes the most barakah-filled step is stepping back.
- **Prioritise the night routine first** — Burnout in the morning usually begins with chaos at night.

Your goal is not intensity — it is continuity.

If You Miss Fajr

Missing Fajr happens, but how you respond determines the direction of your heart.

- **Pray immediately upon waking** — Fulfil the obligation without delay.
- **Do not shame yourself** — Shame kills consistency. Tawbah restores it.
- **Restart that same night** — Fix the night and the morning will follow.
- **Make du'ā' for thabāt (steadfastness)** — Ask Allah for consistency — it is a gift He gives.

Allah looks at your return, not your fall.

Staying awake after Fajr is not just a habit —
It is identity work.

It is you quietly declaring every morning:

**"I choose presence over autopilot.
I choose purpose over drifting.
I choose Allah before the world."**

This is your first act of spiritual leadership each day.
If you master this one habit, the remaining eight flow naturally.
If you neglect it, the others weaken with it.

This is the foundation of a barakah-filled life —
and now you know how to build it.

CHAPTER 5

Habit 2 — Praise & Gratitude: The Language of Barakah

"If you are grateful, I will surely increase you."
— Sūrah Ibrāhīm Q14:7

Gratitude is not a reaction.
It is a position.

In the Qur'an, Allah does not promise increase to effort alone, nor to intensity, nor to ambition. He promises increase to gratitude. Not as a metaphor — as a law.

Barakah does not arrive randomly. It responds to recognition.

When a servant acknowledges the Giver, Allah expands the gift.
When a heart notices blessings, blessings multiply.
When gratitude becomes a habit, increase becomes inevitable.

This is why praise is not postponed until the end of the day.
It is placed at the beginning.

The Prophet ﷺ taught his Ummah to start the morning with al-ḥamd because the first words of the day set the direction of the soul. Gratitude at dawn is not about optimism; it is about alignment — training the heart to see with īmān before the world makes its demands.

This habit does not add time to your morning.
It adds weight to it.

And it begins with the very first breath after waking.

5.1 *The Dawn of Gratitude*

Every sunrise begins with an invitation: *"Say Alhamdulillāh."*

Before you check a phone, stretch, or speak to anyone, the believer's first conversation is with Allah — a quiet acknowledgment:

اَلْحَمْدُ لِلهِ الَّذِي أَحْيَانَا بَعْدَ مَا أَمَاتَنَا وَإِلَيْهِ النُّشُوْرُ

"Alḥamdulillāh alladhī aḥyānā baʿda mā amātanā wa-ilayhi n-nushūr."

"All praise is for You, O Allah, who granted me life after sleep
and to You is my return."

That single phrase reshapes the day. Gratitude at dawn is not a ritual phrase; it's spiritual orientation. It shifts your focus from what is missing to what is present, from anxiety to assurance.

The Prophet ﷺ taught that the morning tongue should begin with praise because the heart follows the tongue. When we start the day praising Allah, we calibrate our soul to reception — we open the gate of *barakah* before anything else enters.

Gratitude is not only a feeling; it's a form of remembrance. Each *Alhamdulillāh* is a soft hammer breaking the walls of heedlessness.

5.2 *Counting Blessings — Not Burdens*

Most people wake counting burdens.
The believer wakes counting blessings.

When Prophet Ayyūb (AS) was tested with illness and loss, he said:

> *"My Lord, harm has touched me, and You are the Most Merciful of the merciful."*
>
> — Sūrah Al-Anbiyā' Q21:83

He didn't hide his pain, yet even in pain his speech began with recognition — *"My Lord."* That single acknowledgment held more *shukr* than a thousand complaints.

Gratitude is not denial; it's definition. You define your world by what you choose to notice.

Notice air in your lungs → peace increases.
Notice your trials → fear increases.

Allah promises *increase* wherever gratitude is planted. If you thank Him for energy, He expands it. If you thank Him for guidance, He deepens it.

You cannot out-praise the Giver; you can only join the chorus of His creation. The birds glorify Him in song, the mountains in echo, the waves in measured rhythm — and the believer with *Alḥamdulillāh.*

The Spiritual Psychology of Contentment

Gratitude dismantles comparison. It transforms scarcity into sufficiency by shifting attention from *what's wrong* to *Who is right there with you.* Modern life whispers *"not enough."* Faith replies *"Alhamdulillāh — more than enough."*

"Look at those below you and not at those above you; that is more likely to make you appreciate the blessings Allah has bestowed upon you."

— Muslim

5.3 *The Science of Shukr*

Allah created gratitude not only as worship but as *healing architecture*.

When you say *Alhamdulillāh* sincerely, you are doing three things simultaneously:

1. Activating the parasympathetic nervous system — heart rate slows, muscles relax.
2. Triggering dopamine and serotonin release — the same chemistry that reduces stress.
3. Re-coding neural focus — your brain literally searches for more things to appreciate.

Studies show that writing or verbalizing gratitude for 21 days increases optimism by 25% and improves sleep quality. Islam had this blueprint 1,400 years ago: the Prophet ﷺ would praise Allah upon waking, upon eating, after sneezing, even after hardship.

This is divine neuroscience — the remembrance of Allah as emotional regulation.

How Gratitude Rewires Belief

Every *Alhamdulillāh* affirms tawḥīd: everything comes from Him.
Every complaint affirms dependence: I am not in control.
Repeated daily, *shukr* rewires your baseline attitude — you stop oscillating between stress and surrender and start living in sakīnah (tranquil awareness).

Gratitude is not what you do when life is good; it is what makes life good.

5.4 *Daily Practice of Praise*

Gratitude is most powerful when it moves from a thought to a routine. You don't wait to "feel thankful." You *train* your heart to remember.

> *"The Prophet ﷺ used to praise Allah in all circumstances."*
> — Muslim

Even in the smallest acts — waking, eating, drinking, dressing — he would begin or end with *Alhamdulillāh*. That is the rhythm we are rebuilding: a heart synchronized with remembrance.

The Morning Praise Routine

1. Upon Waking

Begin with the Prophetic du'ā' of waking:
"Alḥamdulillāh alladhī aḥyānā ba'da mā amātanā wa-ilayhi n-nushūr."

"All praise is for Allah who restored our life after taking it, and to Him is our resurrection."

This sets your heart in gratitude before your feet touch the floor.

2. After Fajr Prayer

Spend a quiet moment in reflection — even 2–3 minutes.
Complete one sentence in a journal or in your mind:

"Today, I thank Allah for..."

Linking gratitude directly after Fajr strengthens presence and intention for the day.

3. While Getting Ready

As you dress, prepare breakfast, or tidy up, name **three blessings aloud**:

- "Alḥamdulillāh for health."

- "Alḥamdulillāh for shelter."
- "Alḥamdulillāh for another chance to do good."

This shifts the mind away from rushing → into conscious awareness.

4. After Eating or Drinking

Begin eating with *"Bismillah."*
After eating say: *"Alḥamdulillāh."*

A simple habit reinforcing that every small blessing is from Him.

5. Starting Your Day's Work / Commute

As you begin your first task — opening your laptop, stepping out of the house, or driving — whisper a small praise:

"Alḥamdulillāh for the ability to work."

This transforms your daily effort into worship.

6. As You Begin Your First Task

Make a discrete intention:
"Yā Allah, I begin in Your name and for Your sake."

Then begin with "Bismillah."
This anchors productivity in barakah.

Start a "99 Days of Praise" page. Each dawn, add one specific mercy — no repeats. By day 99, your lens on life will have permanently shifted.

Gratitude is the heartbeat of remembrance. Miss one beat, and the soul feels faint; revive it, and light rushes back in.

5.5 Praise During Pressure

Saying *Alhamdulillāh* when life is good is instinct.
Saying it when life hurts is faith.

When loss, delay, or humiliation arrives, the believer's first reflex should still be remembrance — not to erase pain, but to anchor perspective. The Prophet ﷺ, after Ṭā'if, when stoned and bleeding, said:

> *"If You are not angry with me, then I do not mind."*

That sentence is the essence of shukr under pressure:

How to Practice Praise in Hardship

1. Name the trial — honesty is not ingratitude.
2. Reaffirm Allah's Names — *Ar-Raḥmān*, *Al-Ḥakīm*, *Al-Ra'ūf* ... He has never stopped being these.
3. Search for the mercy inside the pain — it's often wrapped in delay.
4. Say it aloud: *Alhamdulillāh 'alā kulli ḥāl* — "All praise is due to Allah in every state".
5. Make du'ā' with hope — gratitude doesn't silence need; it dignifies it.

When something pleased him, the Prophet ﷺ would say,

> *"Alhamdulillāh alladhī bi-ni'matihi tatimmu ṣ-ṣāliḥāt."*
>
> "All praise is due to Allah, by whose favour good deeds are accomplished".

He would also show his gratitude by performing a prostration — sujud, to Allah.

When something displeased him, he would say:

> *"Alhamdulillāh 'alā kulli ḥāl."*
> "All praise is to Allah in all circumstances"
>
> — *Ibn Mājah*

A Dua for Pressure

> *Allāhumma inni a'ūdhu bika min qalbin lā yashkur, wa-min nafsin lā tashba', wa-min 'ilmin lā yanfa'.*
>
> "O Allah, I seek refuge in You from a heart that does not show gratitude, a soul that is never satisfied, and knowledge that brings no benefit."

Gratitude under strain is the highest form of surrender; it says, "I trust the Author even when I don't understand the plot."

5.6 Reflection & Re-commitment

The Gratitude Journal Prompt

At the end of each week, write:

> *"This week, I saw Allah's mercy in ...."*
> *"This week, I learned to be thankful for ...."*
> *"Next week, I will praise Him through ...."*

Let these lines become your mirror. Over time, you'll see how divine kindness hides in the ordinary.

The Gratitude Checklist

Practice	**Done**	**Note**
Morning Alhamdulillāh said before phone	☐	
Wrote one line of praise in journal	☐	
Thanked Allah for a small blessing	☐	
Said *Alhamdulillāh ʿalā kulli ḥāl* during stress	☐	
Ended the day with praise	☐	

Tick three daily; barakah will follow.

Closing Duʿāʾ

Alhamdulillāh rabb al-ʿālamīn. Yā Rabb, make my tongue grateful, my heart content, and my days witnesses of Your mercy. Let my praise be a bridge to peace and a light in times of darkness.

Gratitude is the perfume of faith — unseen yet unmistakable. Leave its fragrance wherever you walk.

CHAPTER 6

Habit 3 — Glorify Allah (Tasbīḥ & Dhikr)

"So remember Me; I will remember you."

— *Sūrah Al-Baqarah Q2:152*

Dhikr is not merely a spiritual act; it is an identity. A believer is not defined by wealth, status, or even how much they know — but by how often their heart returns to Allah. If Fajr awakens your body and gratitude awakens your perspective, then **tasbīḥ awakens your soul.**

6.1 Why Tasbīḥ Changes the State of the Heart

The Prophet ﷺ taught that even two simple statements —

"SubḥānAllāhi wa-biḥamdihī, SubḥānAllāhil-'Aẓīm"

are light on the tongue, heavy on the scales, and beloved to the Most Merciful

— Bukhārī, Muslim

That simplicity is the genius of tasbīḥ: it requires nothing but breath, yet it transforms everything inside you.

The Psychological Impact

Modern neuroscience acknowledges a principle that the Prophet ﷺ taught 1,400 years ago: rhythmic remembrance regulates the nervous system.

Repeating "*SubḥānAllāh*" slows the breath, reduces cortisol, and activates the parasympathetic nervous system — the "calm circuit" of the body.

Your brain stops spiraling.
Your thoughts stop racing.
Your heart rate steadies.

Dhikr gives your heart a place to land.

The Spiritual Impact

Glorification lifts you from the weight of your own worries.
When you say *SubḥānAllāh*, you declare:

> "My Lord is perfect. My Lord is above mistakes. My Lord is above limitations."

This one sentence shatters the illusion that your problems are bigger than His Power.

Sheikh Samih explains it beautifully:

"Tasbīḥ stabilizes the heart. It resets your emotional baseline. It pulls you back into a state of tawakkul."

The Practical Impact

A heart that is settled makes better decisions.
A mind that is calm performs better.
A soul that remembers feels lighter and more patient with people.

Dhikr is not an isolated "spiritual break."
It directly affects how you work, think, and show up in the world.

6.2 The Sunnah Dhikr Cycle — Morning, Evening, After Salah

The Prophet ﷺ taught Fāṭimah (ra) a brief dhikr whose impact far outweighed its simplicity.

- SubḥānAllāh — 33 times
- Alḥamdulillāh — 33 times
- Allāhu Akbar — 34 times

He told her:

> *"It is better for you than a servant."*
>
> — Bukhārī

Meaning: *This dhikr will give you a deeper, richer kind of energy than physical assistance ever could.*

Morning Dhikr — *After Fajr*

The morning adhkār protects your day, lifts your mood, and sets your heart in remembrance before the world demands your attention.

Include:

- Ayat al-Kursī
- 3× Sūrat al-Ikhlāṣ, al-Falaq, an-Nās
- "Aṣbaḥnā wa-aṣbaḥa al-mulku lillāh..."
- General praise and gratitude

Morning dhikr is like armour — light entering your chest before the day begins.

Evening Dhikr — *From 'Aṣr*

Evening adhkār soften the heart, calm the mind, and protect you through the night.

Include:

- The same three sūrahs (3× each)
- Ayat al-Kursī
- "Amsaynā wa-amsa al-mulku lillāh..."
- Seeking refuge from evil, harm, and anxieties

Evening dhikr closes the day with peace.

Dhikr After Each Ṣalāh

This is the anchor that ensures your day is punctuated by moments of grounding and clarity.

Sheikh Assim reinforces a valuable point: If you recite the morning/evening adhkār fully, you often "hit two birds with one stone" — the protection of the day and the reward of dhikr after ṣalāh.

The Prophet ﷺ recommended:

- 33× SubḥānAllāh
- 33× Alḥamdulillāh
- 34× Allāhu Akbar
- Followed by the declaration of tawḥīd

This cycle resets your spiritual state, builds consistency, and turns each prayer into a launchpad for the next.

The Power of a Daily Dhikr Routine

When you commit to the Sunnah dhikr cycle, you create a steady spiritual heartbeat:

- Praise in the morning
- Protection in the evening

- Renewal after every prayer
- Strength before sleep

This is barakah in motion — simple actions shifting the inner world.

6.3 The Deep Emotional Impact of "SubḥānAllāh"

Tasbīḥ is not a chant — it is a worldview.

It reframes your problems

When you say *SubḥānAllāh*, you lift your gaze from the problem to the One who can solve it.

You remind yourself:

- My Lord is not limited by my fears.
- My Lord is not constrained by time.
- My Lord is not overwhelmed by the size of my request.

This one remembrance breaks the mental habit of catastrophizing.

It dissolves ego and entitlement

Saying *SubḥānAllāh* frequently softens the heart.
It makes you more patient with people.
It reduces defensiveness.
It clears resentment.

Why? Because glorifying Allah reminds you:

> *"I am a servant. I don't need to control everything."*

It anchors you after emotional storms.

Whether the storm is stress, grief, anger, or frustration — tasbīḥ gives you a reset button.

Even the Prophet ﷺ advise us to repeat "SubḥānAllāh" 100 times a day.

Real-life transformations:

- A young CEO uses tasbīḥ between meetings to reset his nervous system and sharpen focus.
- A mother of three says tasbīḥ quietly while folding laundry — it transformed her irritability into peace.
- A university student does 100 tasbīḥ before studying — and her retention doubled.
- A revert Muslim uses tasbīḥ as their anchor when overwhelmed by change — it grounds them in divine love.

6.4 Tasbīḥ as a Barakah Generator

The Qur'an is direct:

> *"Remember Allah much, that you may prosper."*
>
> — Sūrah Al-Jumu'ah Q62:10

Dhikr is not only spiritually uplifting — it is materially empowering.

When you remember Allah, He remembers you

> *"Fa-udhkuruni adhkurkum washkuru li wa la takfurun."*
>
> *"Remember Me; I will remember you. And thank Me and never be ungrateful."*
>
> — Sūrah Al-Baqarah Q2:152

This is not metaphorical.
It is a divine law.

When Allah "remembers" you:
Doors open.
Hearts soften.
Problems resolve.
Provisions increase.
Opportunities find you.

Morning Dhikr → Better Decisions

Dhikr in the morning aligns the heart with clarity.
And clarity is the foundation of productivity.

Evening Dhikr → Protection of Results

There is no point in gaining during the day if it is not protected at night. Evening dhikr protects:
your wealth
your health
your family
your peace
your progress

Dhikr Lightens Workload

People underestimate this:
A heart that is agitated is less productive.
A heart that is calm is efficient and decisive.

Dhikr opens the mind to creativity, simplifies tasks, and strengthens patience.

6.5 Dhikr Routines for Every Personality Type

Not everyone responds to routine the same way.
This habit is flexible — it adapts to your life.

Structured Dhikr Routine — for Readers Who Prefer Fixed Routines

- 33 SubḥānAllāh
- 33 Alḥamdulillāh
- 34 Allāhu Akbar
- 100 SubḥānAllāh
- Morning adhkār set
- 5-minute silent dhikr walk

Gentle Flow Dhikr — When Your Life Feels Heavy

- Repeat one phrase: SubḥānAllāh
- Whenever anxious, whisper: Allāhu Akbar
- Before bed: 33–33–34

Simple. Effective. Transformative.

On-the-Go Dhikr — for Busy, Active Mornings

- Walking to work
- Waiting at a signal
- Standing in a queue
- Doing chores
- Holding a baby

Dhikr does not require sitting or ritual — it is your heart's constant companion.

Quiet Heart Routine — *for Emotional Days*

When feeling heavy:

- Deep breath
- 10 × "SubḥānAllāh wal-ḥamdulillāh"
- 10 × "Astaghfirullāh"
- 10 × "Allāhu Akbar"
- 1 × heartfelt duʿāʾ

This resets emotional turbulence quickly and gently.

6.6 Reflection & Re-Commitment

Dhikr Habit Checklist

- Said morning adhkār ☐
- Did 33–33–34 after at least one ṣalāh ☐
- Whispered dhikr during stress ☐
- Did an evening remembrance ☐
- Ended the day with Astaghfirullāh ☐

Weekly Reflection Prompt

"What moment this week would have broken me if not for dhikr?"

This reflection teaches the heart gratitude, not just the tongue.

Anchor Supplication

اللَّهُمَّ أَعِنِّيْ عَلَى ذِكْرِكَ وَشُكْرِكَ وَحُسْنِ عِبَادَتِكَ

Allahumma a'inni ala dhikrika, wa shukrika, wa husni 'ibadatika

"O Allah, help me remember You, to be grateful to You, and to worship You in an excellent manner."

— Sunan Abi Dawud

CHAPTER 7

Habit 4 — Recite Qur'an in the Morning

"Indeed, the recitation of Qur'an at dawn is ever witnessed."

— *Sūrah Al-Isrā' Q17:78*

There is a reason the early morning carries a different weight — a quieter stillness, a sharper clarity, a tenderness of the heart you cannot access at any other time of the day. The Qur'ān was revealed in the depth of the night, and the believers who anchor their mornings with its recitation inherit a portion of that light.

The morning is not just "a good time" to recite Qur'ān.
It is *the* time Allah Himself highlights:

"Indeed, the recitation of the Qur'ān at dawn is witnessed."
— *Sūrah Al-Isrā' Q17:78*

Witnessed by who?
By the angels who record your deeds.
By the angels who descend at Fajr.
By Allah, whose attention descends to the lowest heaven at this hour.

This is the moment when heaven leans in.

7.1 — Why the Qur'ān at Dawn Transforms You

1. The Heart Is Softer in the Morning

Before the world enters your mind, before messages, tasks, and noise — your heart is untouched. Whatever enters first shapes the emotional tone of the entire day.

When the first words you hear are the words of Allah, the day aligns around Him.

2. Your Mind Is Clearer

Neurologically, your prefrontal cortex is most receptive after sleep. This is why:

- focus is higher
- retention is stronger
- cravings are lower
- emotional regulation is easier

Morning Qur'ān doesn't only nourish your soul — it improves your psychology.

3. Barakah Flows from the First Act of Obedience

A day that begins with Qur'ān becomes a day protected from misalignment. Recitation is not just ibādah — it is a *direction.*

It orients your heart toward Allah before anything else can claim it.

4. The Qur'ān Sets the Identity of the Day

Everyone has an identity they wake up into:

- worker
- student
- parent

- entrepreneur
- carer
- manager

But the believer chooses a higher identity before all these:
A servant of Allah.
A person of Qur'ān.

Your morning recitation *defines who you are* before the world tells you who to be.

7.2 — The Three Pillars of a Qur'ānic Morning

Recitation • Reflection • Memorisation

To make Qur'ān a morning habit that lasts, the system must be simple and repeatable.

Here is the Barakah Morning model:

Pillar 1 — Recitation —*Tilāwah*

This is the anchor — the act itself.

You can choose one of three pathways:

- Time-based: 5, 10, or 15 minutes
- Page-based: half-page, one page
- Surah-based: one surah per morning

The goal here is *presence*, not performance.

Start small.
Start slow.
Start consistently.

Pillar 2 — Reflection — *Tadabbur*

Reflection is not tafsīr.
Reflection is simply *pausing*.

Ask one question:
"What is Allah teaching me in these āyat today?"

Even a single sentence of reflection can:
stabilise the heart
soothe stress
strengthen gratitude
remind you of your higher purpose

Reflection completes recitation.

Pillar 3 — Memorisation —*Ḥifẓ*

This is your long-term spiritual investment.

The morning is the ideal time:
your tongue is fresh
distractions are low
retention is stronger

Use this simple 3×3 method:

1. Read it 3 times
2. Recite it from memory 3 times
3. Repeat it again after your morning routine

Even a single āyah a day becomes 365 āyāt a year.

7.3 — Your 10-Minute Qur'ān Plan —Beginner-Friendly

Designed for busy professionals, parents, and students.

Minute 1: Bismillah + focus
Minutes 2–6: Recite one page (or half-page)
Minute 7: Reflect — write one sentence
Minutes 8–10: Memorise 1 line

This is your minimum viable Qur'ān habit.

It works.

7.4 — The Qur'ān Ladder — Choose Your Level

Level 1 — The Starter (5 minutes)

- Recite 5 lines
- Reflect with one question
- Memorise one phrase

Level 2 — The Builder (10–15 minutes)

- Recite 1 page
- Reflect one sentence
- Memorise 1–2 āyāt

Level 3 — The Committed (20–30 minutes)

- Recite 2 pages
- Reflect deeply
- Memorise 3–4 āyāt

Level 4 — The Qur'ān Person (45–60 minutes)

- 1 hizb or longer
- Journal reflections
- Active long-term memorisation

You choose the level;
consistency chooses the results.

7.5 — Reflection Prompts That Open the Heart

Choose one per day:

- "What attribute of Allah appears in this āyah?"
- "What action is Allah calling me toward?"
- "What comfort is hidden here for me?"
- "What warning is Allah protecting me from?"

These turn the Qur'ān into a conversation — not a task.

7.6 — Troubleshooting: When It Gets Hard

If you feel sleepy

- recite standing
- recite with soft voice
- open a window

If you feel overwhelmed

- reduce the pages
- read only familiar surahs
- start with shorter portions

If you miss a morning

- do not shame yourself
- recite a shorter portion later
- restart the next day with intention

Your goal is consistency, not perfection.

7.7 — Real Qur'ān Morning Templates for Real Lives

The Busy Parent

- Fajr
- 5-minute recitation
- 1 āyah memorisation
- 1-line reflection
- Begin breakfast

The Student

- Fajr
- Review yesterday's memorisation
- New 1–2 āyāt
- Recitation during sunrise
- Quick reflection before lectures

The Professional

- Fajr
- 1 page recitation
- 1 āyah memorisation
- Reflection during commute
- Begin deep work

- Fajr
- Tilāwah on prayer mat
- Tadabbur journaling
- 10-minute memorisation
- Begin strategy work

7.8 — Why This Habit Unlocks Barakah

Because the Qur'ān is not only guidance — **it is barakah itself**.

Allah does not describe the Qur'ān merely as instruction or inspiration. He names it directly:

> *"And this is a blessed Book which We have sent down..."*
>
> — Sūrah Al-An'ām Q6:155

Barakah is not something we bring *to* the Qur'ān by reading it. Barakah flows *from* the Qur'ān into the one who approaches it.

That is why the Qur'ān nourishes what modern systems try to manage:

- It calms anxiety by anchoring the heart in remembrance
- It strengthens focus by disciplining the mind
- It expands gratitude by realigning perception
- It regulates emotions by restoring inner order
- It sharpens purpose by clarifying direction
- It anchors you in tawakkul, not control

When the Qur'ān enters the morning, disorder leaves.

This is why the Prophet ﷺ and the earliest generations treated Qur'ān at the start of the day not as a task, but as a **foundation**. The heart takes its tone from its first input. What enters first, governs what follows.

The morning Qur'ān habit is the one habit that makes all the others easier.
It steadies dhikr.
It deepens du'ā'.
It softens discipline into devotion.

It is the core of *The Barakah Morning*.

A day that begins with Qur'ān does not begin with you —
it begins with Allah.

This is the secret of barakah.

Let the Qur'ān be your first light,
and watch how Allah becomes the Light of your entire life.

CHAPTER 8

Habit 5 — Send Ṣalawāt on the Prophet ﷺ

Fill Your Morning with Mercy

There is a unique fragrance that enters the life of a believer who regularly sends ṣalawāt upon the Prophet ﷺ. It is a habit that takes seconds, yet it draws mercy, removes burdens, lifts the heart, and brings a sense of calm unmatched by anything else.

If the Qur'ān nourishes the morning, then ṣalawāt softens it.
If Qur'ān anchors the heart, ṣalawāt warms it.

The Prophet ﷺ said:

> *"Whoever sends one blessing upon me, Allah sends ten blessings upon him."*
>
> — Muslim

Ten mercies.
Ten protections.
Ten openings.
Ten elevations.
For each single ṣalāh you send.

There is no investment on earth with a return like this.

8.1 — Why Ṣalawāt Belongs in the Morning

1. It Calms the Emotional System

Modern psychology explains that repetitive, heart-centred phrases lower cortisol, reduce anxiety, and improve emotional regulation.

Ṣalawāt is dhikr — but dhikr tied to *love.*
It softens stress from the root, not just the symptoms.

2. It Connects You to the Best Example

The morning is when you set your identity for the day.
Sending ṣalawāt reminds you of:

- character
- patience
- excellence
- truthfulness
- self-discipline
- mercy toward others

It is identity-shaping.

3. It Opens the Doors of Barakah

The Prophet ﷺ said:

> *"The closest people to me on the Day of Judgment are those who send the most ṣalawāt upon me."*
> — Tirmidhī

Proximity to the Messenger ﷺ is proximity to barakah.

Your morning feels different, flows differently, and unfolds differently when it begins with ṣalawāt.

4. It Uplifts You When You Are Low

Many people wake up with emotional heaviness:

- unfinished tasks
- fear of the day
- sadness
- stress
- guilt

Ṣalawāt resets the emotional climate.

It is spiritual first-aid.

8.2 — The Sunnah of Sending Ṣalawāt

The Prophet ﷺ encouraged frequent ṣalawāt — morning, evening, and in moments of need.

The most complete form is *Ṣalāt Ibrāhīmiyyah*:

> *Allāhumma ṣalli ʿalā Muḥammad wa ʿalā āli Muḥammad, kamā ṣallayta ʿalā Ibrāhīma wa ʿalā āli Ibrāhīm, innaka Ḥamīdu-m-Majīd, Allāhumma bārik ʿalā Muḥammad, wa ʿalā āli Muḥammad, kamā bārakta ʿalā Ibrāhīma wa ʿalā āli Ibrāhīm, innaka Ḥamīdu-m-Majīd.*
>
> O Allah, honour and have mercy upon Muhammad and the family of Muhammad as You have honoured and had mercy upon Ibrāhīm and the family of Ibrāhīm. Indeed, You are the Most Praiseworthy, the Most Glorious. O Allah, bless Muhammad and the family of Muhammad as You have blessed Ibrāhīm and the family of Ibrāhīm. Indeed, You are the Most Praiseworthy, the Most Glorious.

A shorter version:

Allāhumma ṣalli ʿalā Muḥammad wa ʿalā āli Muḥammad.

Both count.
Both carry reward.
Both transform your state.

8.3 — The 3 Forms of Morning Ṣalawāt

A simple system you can repeat every day

Form 1 — Soft Flow (1–2 minutes)

Perfect for starting the morning gently.

Repeat softly for one minute:
Allāhumma ṣalli ʿalā Muḥammad wa ʿalā āli Muḥammad.

This alone brings light.

Form 2 — Focused Flow (33× Model)

Mirrors the rhythm of morning adhkār.

- 11 × Ṣallallāhu ʿalā Muḥammad
- 11 × Allāhumma ṣalli ʿalā Muḥammad
- 11 × Ṣallallāhu ʿalayhi wa sallam

This builds emotional presence and rhythm.

Form 3 — Deep Flow (Ṣalāt Ibrāhīmiyyah)

One recitation with full presence:

Allāhumma ṣalli ʿalā Muḥammad wa ʿalā āli Muḥammad, kamā ṣallayta ʿalā Ibrāhīma wa ʿalā āli Ibrāhīm, innaka Ḥamīdu-m-Majīd, Allāhumma bārik ʿalā Muḥammad, wa ʿalā āli Muḥammad, kamā bārakta ʿalā Ibrāhīma wa ʿalā āli Ibrāhīm, innaka Ḥamīdu-m-Majīd.

This is the highest form of ṣalawāt — the one you recite in tashahhud, and the one the Prophet ﷺ taught directly.

Abd al-Raḥmān ibn Abī Laylā (raḥimahullāh) said: "Ka'b ibn 'Ujrah (raḍiy Allāhu 'anhu) met me and said: 'Shall I not give you a gift I received from the Messenger of Allah ﷺ?' I replied: 'Yes of course, gift it to me.' So, he said: 'We asked the Messenger of Allah ﷺ: "O Messenger of Allah ﷺ, how should we invoke ṣalāh upon you, the members of the family, for Allah has taught us how to send salām upon you?" He ﷺ replied: "Say: [the above]."

— Bukhārī 3370

8.4 — Integrating Ṣalawāt Into the Barakah Morning Routine

Your goal is not repetition — but rhythm.
Make ṣalawāt flow naturally in the quiet moments of your morning.

A simple sequence:

1. Upon waking: 3–5 ṣalawāt
2. After Fajr: 10–33 ṣalawāt
3. While getting ready: soft ṣalawāt under your breath
4. Before starting work: 7 ṣalawāt
5. During commute: continuous light ṣalawāt

The point is continuity, not intensity.

8.5 — Ṣalawāt for Different Lifestyles

The Busy Parent

- After settling the children
- 10 ṣalawāt while preparing breakfast
- One Ṣalāt Ibrāhīmiyyah before leaving home

Why it works:
Grounds you before the day becomes chaotic.

The Professional

- 33 ṣalawāt in commute or walking to transport
- 3 ṣalawāt before starting the first task

Why it works:
Resets mindset, reduces work pressure.

The Student

- 1–2 minutes ṣalawāt after Fajr
- 10 ṣalawāt before entering class
- Soft ṣalawāt during breaks

Why it works:
Improves focus and reduces anxiety.

The Entrepreneur

- 33 ṣalawāt before planning
- Ṣalāt Ibrāhīmiyyah before meetings
- Light ṣalawāt during strategy deep work

Why it works:
Aligns decisions with clarity and humility.

8.6 — Micro Moments for Ṣalawāt

These tiny cues help build the habit:

- every time you feel a burst of stress
- before sending a message

- while waiting for loading screens
- while tying your shoes
- when you remember a blessing
- before answering a phone call
- when you enter or leave your house
- before eating

These transform ordinary moments into spiritual elevation.

8.7 — Troubleshooting: When It Feels Hard

If you forget

Use environmental cues:

- sticky note
- lock screen reminder
- dua card

If your heart feels disconnected

Slow the pace
Say it softly
Imagine the Prophet ﷺ receiving your blessings
Remember his sacrifices for you

If you feel rushed

Do just 3 ṣalawāt
Small is still rewarded
The key is consistency

If you feel guilty for inconsistency

Remember:
Even *one* ṣalāh is multiplied by *ten*.
Allah is generous with the little you do.

8.8 — The Identity of "A Person of Ṣalawāt"

Eventually, ṣalawāt becomes more than a habit.
It becomes *who you are*.

A person:
whose heart is softened
whose words are gentle
whose mornings are blessed
whose anxieties are calmed
whose day flows with mercy
whose heart is connected to the Messenger ﷺ

This identity changes your character, not just your routine.

Ṣalawāt is not a small act. It is one of the most powerful ways to draw the mercy of Allah into your morning.

When you send blessings upon the Prophet ﷺ, Allah sends blessings upon you — tenfold, every single time.

Let your morning be wrapped in mercy.
Let your heart be warmed by love.
Let your day begin with the remembrance of the one who brought you guidance.

This is the Barakah Morning.

CHAPTER 9

Habit 6 — Make Istighfār

Clear Your Heart, Clear Your Morning

There is a subtle heaviness many people wake up with.
Not always sadness.
Not always stress.

Sometimes...it is just *weight.*
A tightness in the chest.
A fog in the mind.
A feeling of pressure, guilt, or unease.

Often, this heaviness comes from unseen emotional or spiritual residue — moments from yesterday we regret, words we wish we could take back, obligations we delayed, sins we minimised, or hearts we unsettled.

Out of His mercy, Allah did not leave the believer to carry this weight into a new day.

He gifted us a daily spiritual cleanser:

Istighfār — seeking forgiveness.

It dissolves heaviness.
It resets the heart.
It removes unseen barriers to barakah.

And the Qur'an makes something strikingly clear:
this cleansing was meant to happen early.

Allah praises the believers not only for their prayer or patience — but for what they do **before the day begins**:

"And in the hours before dawn, they would seek forgiveness."
— Surat adh-Dhāriyāt, Q51:18

Istighfār in the morning is not accidental.
It is strategic mercy.

Before the mind fills with tasks,
before the heart is pulled by demands,
before the soul is tested by the world,
Allah invites you to clear what remains from yesterday.

The Prophet ﷺ embodied this habit daily. He said:

> *"By Allah, I seek forgiveness from Allah and repent to Him more than seventy times a day."*

— Ṣaḥīḥ al-Bukhārī

This is not excessive guilt.
This is **emotional and spiritual hygiene**.

9.1 — Why Istighfār Belongs in the Morning

1. It Lightens the Heart

Istighfār clears the emotional fog you woke up with.

It dissolves the residue of yesterday — the stress, the heaviness, the missteps, the moments you wish had unfolded differently.

Every quiet ***"Astaghfirullāh"*** lifts a weight you may not even realise you're carrying.

Your chest softens.
Your breath deepens.
Your heart becomes lighter, ready to receive barakah for the day ahead.

This is how you step into the morning **unburdened**, cleansed, and spiritually renewed.

2. It Opens Doors You Cannot See

Allah says:

> *"Seek forgiveness from your Lord...*
> *He will send rain upon you in abundance,*
> *grant you wealth and children,*
> *and provide for you gardens and rivers."*
> — Surat Nūḥ, Q71:10–12

Istighfār is not a passive act. It is a **door-opener**, a **barakah generator**, a spiritual force that shifts what happens in your day before you even step into it.

Opportunities soften.
Paths widen.
Hardships ease.
Provision flows from directions you never anticipated.

When you seek forgiveness in the morning, you are not only clearing the past — you are **unlocking the day in front of you**.

3. It Protects You from Your Own Mistakes

You will slip.
You will forget.
Your heart will rise and fall — this is the nature of being human.

Istighfār in the morning places a shield around you before the day accelerates. It resets your spiritual state *before* you enter conversations, decisions, temptations, and stresses that could pull you off-centre.

It is Allah's way of saying:
"Begin clean, and I will guard you as you go."

When you start your morning with forgiveness, you walk into the day protected from the mistakes you haven't made yet.

4. It Softens the Spiritual Body

Just as your physical body needs stretching to move with ease, your *spiritual body* needs istighfār to soften and awaken.

Istighfār makes your heart receptive to:

- Qur'ān
- du'ā'
- ṣalawāt
- mercy
- clarity

When the heart is hard, all of these become difficult —
the Qur'an feels distant, du'ā' feels heavy, and even simple acts of worship require effort.

A few sincere moments of ***"Astaghfirullāh"*** soften the inner world. They make your heart flexible, open, and ready to receive what Allah wants to place within it.

Istighfār prepares you to benefit from everything that comes after.

9.2 — *The Psychology of Istighfār*

Istighfār doesn't only cleanse the soul — it recalibrates the mind. Its psychological impact is immediate, measurable, and profound.

Calms Anxiety

Repeating a grounding phrase slows your breathing, steadies your heartbeat, and signals the nervous system to relax. Your anxiety drops, and your inner world quiets.

Reduces Guilt and Mental Noise

Instead of replaying mistakes in your mind, istighfār turns regret into repentance — and repentance into relief. The mental noise softens, and you stop carrying yesterday into today.

Strengthens Self-Awareness

Istighfār helps you recognise your flaws gently, without spiralling into shame. It teaches you to see yourself honestly *and* compassionately.

Builds Humility

A heart that says "*Astaghfirullāh*" regularly becomes soft, teachable, and receptive. Humility improves every area of your life — you learn faster, apologise faster, forgive faster, and love deeper.

Istighfār regulates you emotionally before the world has a chance to destabilise you. It prepares your heart for clarity, productivity, and connection.

9.3 — The Types of Morning Istighfār

The heart does not need one form of forgiveness —
it needs **different kinds of cleansing at different moments**.

Sometimes it needs softening.
Sometimes focus.
Sometimes full return.

These forms of istighfār are not competing practices. Together, they form a **complete morning system** — restoring calm, clarity, and spiritual alignment before the day begins.

Type 1 — Soft Istighfār — *for calm*

The heart does not need one form of forgiveness —
it needs **different kinds of cleansing at different moments**.

Sometimes it needs softening.
Sometimes focus.
Sometimes full return.

These forms of istighfār are not competing practices. Together, they form a **complete morning system** — restoring calm, clarity, and spiritual alignment before the day begins.

Type 2 — Structured Istighfār — *33× Model*

Use this after your morning adhkār to bring focus and intentionality.

Recite:
33 × *"Astaghfirullāh"*

Then pause.
Take one slow, grounding breath.

And quietly say:

"O Allah, forgive me in what I know and in what I do not know."

This keeps istighfār expansive, not restrictive.

It transforms forgiveness from a reaction into a posture — one of humility, awareness, and surrender. Over time, this practice softens the heart, sharpens self-awareness without self-blame, and creates emotional clarity that carries into the day.

Type 3 — Deep Istighfār —*Sayyid al-Istighfār*

This is the most complete, powerful form of repentance — a full return to Allah with honesty, humility, and hope.

Recite:

اَللّٰهُمَّ أَنْتَ رَبِّيْ لَا إِلٰهَ إِلَّا أَنْتَ ، خَلَقْتَنِيْ وَأَنَا عَبْدُكَ ، وَأَنَا
عَلَىٰ عَهْدِكَ وَوَعْدِكَ مَا اسْتَطَعْتُ ، أَعُوْذُ بِكَ مِنْ شَرِّ مَا
صَنَعْتُ ، أَبُوْءُ لَكَ بِنِعْمَتِكَ عَلَيَّ وَأَبُوْءُ بِذَنْبِيْ ، فَاغْفِرْ لِيْ
فَإِنَّهُ لَا يَغْفِرُ الذُّنُوْبَ إِلَّا أَنْتَ

Allāhumma Anta Rabbī, lā ilāha illā Ant, khalaqtanī wa ana ʿabduk, wa ana ʿalā ʿahdika wa waʿdika mā'staṭaʿt, aʿūdhu bika min sharri mā ṣanaʿt, abū'u laka bi niʿmatika ʿalayya wa abū'u bi-dhambī fa-ghfir lī fa-innahū lā yaghfiru-dh-dhunūba illā Ant.

O Allah, You are my Lord. There is no god except You.
You created me, and I am Your servant.
I remain upon Your covenant and promise as best as I can.
I seek refuge in You from the evil I have done.
I acknowledge Your blessings upon me, and I confess my sins.
So, forgive me, for none forgives sins except You.

This is the highest form of seeking forgiveness — a complete return to Allah with sincerity, trust, and dependence.

The Power of the Three Types

Use one type on busy days.
Use all three on heavy days.
Rotate them as your heart requires.

Together, they:
calm your heart
clean your inner world
open doors of barakah
reset your relationship with Allah
prepare your soul for Qur'ān, work, and worship

This is not sporadic repentance.
This is **forgiveness as a morning discipline**.

And when forgiveness becomes disciplined,
barakah follows naturally.

9.4 — *Where Istighfār Fits in the Barakah Morning*

Istighfār has *multiple* powerful times — but the morning carries a special spiritual weight.

Here is how it fits into your Barakah Morning, based on authentic sources:

1. The Best Time: Before Fajr — *Last Third of the Night*

The **highest** time for istighfār is the last third of the night — the hours just before Fajr.

Allah praises the believers who:

> *"...seek forgiveness in the early dawn."*
>
> — Sūrah Adh-Dhāriyāt Q51:18
>
> And the Prophet ﷺ told us that in this window, Allah descends and calls:
>
> "Who is seeking My forgiveness so I may forgive him?"
>
> — Bukhari & Muslim

If you wake before Fajr — even briefly — this is your moment for deep, quiet istighfār.

But if you don't wake up early?
Don't worry — the morning still has powerful openings for you.

2. After Fajr: Morning Adhkār → Then Istighfār

Once you pray Fajr, your structured morning begins.

The sequence is simple:

Step 1 — Morning Adhkār (Sunnah priority)

These are your spiritual shield and your daily grounding.

Step 2 — Istighfār

Right *after* your adhkār is a beautiful place for:

- soft istighfār
- structured istighfār
- Sayyid al-Istighfār

This is where you clear your emotional slate, soften your heart, and prepare your soul to receive Qur'ān.

This is istighfār as a **spiritual reset button** for your morning.

3. After Istighfār: Qur'ān Recitation

A heart softened by istighfār becomes:
more receptive to Qur'ān
more focused
less distracted
more emotionally open

Istighfār prepares the soil;
Qur'ān plants the seeds.

4. After Qur'ān: Ṣalawāt

Once your heart is warmed,
send ṣalawāt upon the Prophet ﷺ.

It draws mercy, increases blessings, and seals your morning worship with light.

5. Throughout the Day

You can repeat istighfār:

- after prayers
- when you slip or feel regret
- during moments of stress
- while walking or commuting
- silently throughout your tasks

The Prophet ﷺ made istighfār **about 70–100 times a day**, despite being sinless — because istighfār is not only forgiveness; it is closeness.

Your Barakah Morning Flow — *Authentic Sequence*

Before Fajr *(if awake)*:
Deep istighfār — the most powerful time of all.

After Fajr:

1. Morning Adhkār
2. Istighfār
3. Qur'ān recitation
4. Ṣalawāt
5. Begin your morning tasks

This is the flow that aligns your heart with mercy, your mind with clarity, and your day with barakah.

9.5 — Real-Life Templates

The Busy Parent

- 10 istighfār after Fajr
- 33 istighfār while preparing breakfast
- Soft istighfār when feeling overwhelmed

The Professional

- 10 istighfār before opening the laptop
- 3 istighfār before each major task
- 33 istighfār on commute home

The Student

- 1-minute istighfār before reviewing notes
- 3–7 istighfār before entering class
- Sayyid al-Istighfār before sleep

The Entrepreneur

- 33 istighfār before planning
- 3 istighfār before each meeting
- Soft istighfār during strategy blocks

9.6 — Micro-Moments of Istighfār

These tiny cues help build an automatic habit:

- when you feel stress rising
- when you mis-speak
- when you pause between tasks
- while waiting for your kettle
- before sending a message
- after a negative emotion
- when you step outside

- before replying to someone

These small acts create a spiritual rhythm throughout the day.

9.7 — Troubleshooting

If it feels repetitive

Slow down.
Say it with presence.
Imagine the forgiveness entering your heart.

If it feels meaningless

Tie each "Astaghfirullāh" to one area of your life:

- patience
- anger
- mistakes
- missed opportunities

If you feel guilty

Remember: guilt is not a destination — it is a *signal.*
Allah already knows your flaws.
Istighfār is your return, not your punishment.

If you forget

Pair it with existing routines:

- after Qur'ān
- after ṣalawāt
- before starting work

9.8 — The Identity of a Person of Istighfār

When you become a person of istighfār, something inside you shifts.

You feel:

- lighter
- calmer
- softer
- more reflective
- less reactive
- more grounded
- closer to Allah

Your heart clears.
Your day flows with more ease.
Your mistakes stop imprisoning you — they become pathways that lead you back to Allah.

This is what barakah feels like:
a quiet, steady lightness that follows you into every task.

Istighfār is not a small habit.
It is a spiritual cleansing, a recalibration of the heart, a direct request for divine mercy. It reshapes your inner world long before it changes your outer one.

Sometimes a single
"Astaghfirullāh"
can lift a burden you could not lift on your own.

So let your morning begin with release, not pressure.
With forgiveness, not guilt.

With lightness, not heaviness.
With a heart that knows its Lord and returns to Him with hope.

This is Habit 6.
This is the Barakah Morning.

CHAPTER 10

Habit 7 — Salatu Duḥā

The Quiet Prayer of Provision, Calm, and Expansion

There is a salah many Muslims know *about*,
but few Muslims *live with*.
A prayer that carries unusual softness, unusual barakah, and unusual effect on the day.

That prayer is **Duḥā** —
the forenoon salah prayed after sunrise and before *Zhur*.

The Prophet ﷺ described it in a way that makes you realise
this is not an "extra prayer."

It is **a gift**,
a cleanser,
a source of rizq,
a form of gratitude,
and a spiritual reset in the middle of your morning.

He ﷺ said:

> *"In the morning, charity is due on every joint of your body.*
> *But every tasbīḥah is charity, every takbīrah is charity...*
> *and two rak'ahs of Duḥā suffice for all of that."*
>
> — Muslim

Two rak'ahs — replacing over **360 acts of charity**.

This is divine generosity.

10.1 — What Is Salatu Duḥā Exactly?

- It is a voluntary prayer
- prayed after the sun fully rises
- and before Zhur enters
- best known for attracting rizq, relief, and spiritual expansion

It takes **2–8 rak'ahs**, depending on your time.

If you pray only **two**, you fulfil the hadith above.
If you pray **four**, you follow the extended sunnah.
If you pray **eight**, you follow the practice of the most spiritually ambitious companions.

But even **two** carry weight.

10.2 — Why This Prayer Matters for a Barakah Morning

Most people rush through their morning.
By mid-morning, stress, speed, and pressure start to build.

Duḥā interrupts that cycle.

It slows you down.
It resets the heart.
It protects your rizq.
It softens the next phase of the day.

Allah's Messenger ﷺ narrated that Allah the Most High said:

> *"Son of Adam: Perform four Rak'at for Me in the beginning of the day (Duha); it will suffice you for the latter part of the day."*
>
> — Tirmidhī

This is not poetic.
It is a promise.

Duḥā is Allah saying:
"Give Me a small window in the morning —
and I will take care of the rest."

10.3 — The Rizq Expansion Effect

From the earliest generations, Duḥā has been known as the **prayer of provision**.

Ibn al-Qayyim describes Salat ad-Duḥā as a worship that:

- attracts provision (rizq)
- preserves health
- repels harm and illness
- opens the pathways of sustenance

He writes that the morning hours — when kept alive by this prayer — have a unique spiritual effect in drawing ease, blessing, and expansion into your day.

1. A Source of Provision and Ease

Duḥā opens doors you cannot see. It brings softness into people's hearts, ease in transactions, and clarity in decisions. It unties knots in your morning and clears obstacles before they appear.

2. A Form of Daily Charity

The Prophet ﷺ taught that every joint in your body owes a charity each morning — and that **Duḥā replaces all of them**.

It is worship that fulfils your body's rights while multiplying your blessings.

3. A Sunnah of Expansion

Duḥā is a Sunnah Mu'akkadah — a highly encouraged practice the Prophet ﷺ prayed regularly and advised his companions to maintain. Its consistent performance is linked with:

- forgiveness
- protection
- stability
- material ease
- spiritual uplift

4. The Spirit of Surah Ad-Duḥā

And perhaps the greatest proof of Duḥā's connection to provision is Surah 93 — **Ad-Duḥā**.

A surah in which Allah reminds the Prophet ﷺ:

- of past provisions
- of current care
- of future expansion

A surah of comfort.
A surah of reassurance.
A surah of rising after heaviness.

When you pray Duḥā, you align your morning with the spirit of that surah — a promise that what lies ahead is better than what came before.

10.4 — The Emotional Healing Effect

Duḥā is not only about money and opportunities.
It is also about *healing*.

The Prophet ﷺ said Allah loves:

- those who remember Him in calm,
- and those who remember Him in difficulty.

Duḥā is prayed when the world is awake,
but your heart wants a moment of silence.

It becomes:

- a pause from noise
- a breath from pressure
- a sanctuary from rush
- a moment of softness with Allah

For many, Duḥā becomes their daily calm.

10.5 — Timing: The Optimal Window

Duḥā is flexible — but it also has an optimal range that carries immense spiritual weight.

Start:

12–15 minutes after sunrise — *when the sun has fully risen*

End:

10–15 minutes before Dhuhr
Within this window, you choose the level your day can hold.
Each version carries its own barakah.

1. Soft Duḥā — *Quick & Light*

Perfect for busy mornings or when you simply want to stay consistent.

- 2 rakʿahs
- any short sūrahs
- slow, intentional breathing

This is your spiritual "check-in" — enough to unlock the blessings of Duḥā without demanding time you don't have.

Even on your hardest days, Soft Duḥā keeps the door of provision open.

2. Deep Duḥā— Reflective & Steady

A beautiful pairing with your Qur'ān time or reflection routines.

- 4 rakʿahs
- a calmer, slower pace
- time for sincere duʿāʾ between units

This is the Duḥā that soothes the heart, expands clarity, and fills the morning with sakīnah. It's the prayer of expansion in both rizq and tranquility.

3. Stretch Duḥā — *For Big Needs & Big Breakthroughs*

For moments when you need extra support, deeper ease, or a major opening from Allah.

- 8 rakʿahs
- often prayed by those facing decisions, challenges, or seeking a breakthrough

This is the Duḥā of people who are asking Allah for something *big*. It stretches the heart, the intention, and the hope.

Duḥā Adapts to Your Season of Life

Some mornings you will have 2 minutes.
Some mornings you will have 20.
Some seasons allow 2 rak'ahs,
Other seasons allow 8.

Duḥā meets you where you are —
and brings barakah to whatever your morning can hold.

10.6 — How to Pray Duḥā (Simple Guide)

Salatu Duḥā is one of the most flexible, uplifting, and spiritually potent Sunnah prayers. It is easy to perform, yet its rewards ripple through your entire day.

Here's how to pray it — and why it carries so much barakah.

How Many Rak'ahs?

Minimum: 2 rak'ahs
This is the foundation of Duḥā. Even on your busiest mornings, two units unlock the reward.

Virtues of 2 Rak'ahs:

- It counts as charity for all 360 joints in your body for that day. (The Prophet ﷺ explicitly mentioned this.)
- The Prophet ﷺ advised Abū Hurayrah to pray two rak'ahs of Duḥā daily and never abandon it.
- If you remain in your prayer spot after Fajr, remembering Allah until sunrise and then pray Duḥā, you receive the reward of a complete Hajj and 'Umrah — perfect, perfect, perfect.
  — Tirmidhi

Even the minimum carries maximum blessing.

Recommended: 4 rak'ahs
This is the level the Prophet ﷺ encouraged often — steady, balanced, and deeply nourishing.

Maximum reported: **8 rak'ahs**
Prayed by those seeking deeper expansion, breakthrough, or protection.

Salatu Duḥā adapts to your day and your capacity.

What to Recite?

There is **no specific sūrah required**, which makes this prayer beautifully accessible. Allah is looking at your sincerity, not your sequence.
Your presence matters more than the pace or the length of your recitation.

The Essence of Duḥā

Duḥā is simple.
Soft.
Light.
And yet it unlocks a day full of protection, clarity, ease, and provision.

Even two rak'ahs can change the texture of your morning.
Four can transform your entire day.
Eight can shift the course of your life.

10.7 — The Duḥā Mindset — Before You Begin

Before you rise for Duḥā, pause.
Take one quiet breath.
And hand your entire morning over to Allah.

Say in your heart:

> *"Yā Allah, I give You my morning. Take care of what I can see and what I cannot see."*

This intention changes everything.

Duḥā is not just something you *do*.
It is something you *receive*.

When your mindset is one of trust, openness, and reliance, the prayer becomes more than rakʿahs — it becomes an invitation for Allah to expand your day, your provision, your clarity, and your heart.

This is how you don't just *pray* Duḥā.
You **live** Duḥā.

10.8 — Real-Life Routines

Duḥā is a prayer that adapts to your life.
Here's how it fits into different real-world mornings — simply, naturally, and without pressure.

The Busy Professional

Arrive at work ten minutes early.
Slip into a quiet meeting room.
Pray **2 rakʿahs** before opening your laptop.

Duḥā becomes the boundary between the outside world and your inner world — a spiritual buffer that grounds your mind before the day accelerates.

The Parent

Once the school run is done and your home is quiet again,
pray Duḥā before diving into the next round of responsibilities.

It becomes your moment of stillness — a breath of sakīnah after a busy morning of caring for others.

The Student

Between classes or during a study break,
pray **2** or **4 rak'ahs** to reset your mind, sharpen focus, and steady your emotions.

Duḥā clears cognitive fog and helps anchor your academic day in barakah.

The Entrepreneur

After your morning deep-work block, use Duḥā as your **reset ritual.2** or **4 rak'ahs** help you shift gears, regain clarity, and reconnect with purpose before moving into meetings, decisions, or planning.

The Homemaker

Once the morning chores settle and the home is calm, pray Duḥā as your personal pause — a moment that reminds you that your soul needs tending just as much as your home.

This prayer becomes your replenishment.

The Traveller

In a hotel room, a quiet corner of the masjid, or after breakfast on the road — Duḥā travels with you.

It adjusts to the rhythm of your journey and keeps your heart connected even when your routine is disrupted.

Wherever life takes you, Duḥā goes too.

10.9 — Troubleshooting

"I forget."

Tie it to a fixed action:

- after breakfast
- after commute
- after school drop-off

"I feel nothing."

Duḥā is a slow-blooming habit.
Some days feel empty —
but spiritually, nothing is ever wasted.

"My morning is too busy."

Two rakʿahs take about 2 - 3 minutes.
If you have time to scroll, you have time for Duḥā.

"I overslept and missed Fajr."

Still pray Duḥā.
It is independent of Fajr.

10.10 — The Identity Shift

When Salatu Duḥā becomes part of your morning, it doesn't just change your schedule — **it changes you.**

You begin to notice that you are:

- softer in your responses
- calmer under pressure
- more trusting of Allah
- less reactive to difficulty
- more productive with less effort
- more focused with less noise
- more spiritually anchored in every decision

Your morning stops feeling chaotic.
It becomes **curated**, intentional, and spiritually supported.

This is the inner engineering of barakah.

Salatu Duḥā is a small prayer with a **large impact** —
a quiet act with a **loud effect** —
a few minutes of stillness that **reorders your entire morning**.

This is Habit 7:
the prayer that unlocks provision, clarity, and emotional ease.

And once you build Salatu Duḥā into your morning rhythm, the shift is so clear, so tangible, so grounding that you'll genuinely wonder how you ever lived without it.

CHAPTER 11

Habit 8 — Make Du'ā'

Turning Your Mornings into Conversations with Allah

There is a moment after Fajr when the world is quiet,
your mind is clear,
your heart is soft,
and your soul is closest to truth.

This is the moment du'ā' becomes different.

Not rushed.
Not distracted.
Not a checklist.

But a *conversation* — with the One who already knows your needs,
your fears,
your hopes,
and your future.

The morning du'ā' is not an extra ritual.
It is the engine of barakah.

The Prophet ﷺ said:

"Du'ā' is worship."

—Tirmidhī

And another narration:

"Your Lord is Generous and Shy.
When His servant raises his hands to Him,

He feels shy to return them empty."

— Abū Dāwūd

This is the intimate nature of du'ā' —
Pure generosity from Allah.
Pure vulnerability from you.

11.1 — Why Du'ā' Hits Harder in the Morning

1. Your heart is naturally soft after sleep.
You have not yet been exposed to noise, stress, people, or pressure.

2. The angels witness the Fajr time.
Your words land differently in the unseen world.

3. The Prophet ﷺ made powerful morning du'ā's.
He anchored his day with intention, surrender, and hope.

4. Your mind is clearer.
You see your life with honesty — not panic.

5. Morning du'ā' shapes the day ahead.
It is you saying: *"Yā Allah, don't let me walk today alone."*

11.2 — The Structure of a Powerful Du'ā'

Du'ā' is simple — but a *powerful* du'ā' follows a structure the Prophet ﷺ consistently taught. When these elements come together, your words carry sincerity, depth, humility and a stronger path to acceptance.

Below is the complete du'ā' framework.

1. Begin by Praising and Glorifying Allah

The Prophet ﷺ once saw a man making du'ā' without first praising Allah, and he said the man had been *hasty*. This moment became a foundational teaching:

a complete du'ā' must begin with praising Allah.

Before any request, before any need, before any tear, the heart must stand in recognition of who Allah is. This is not a formality — it is the key that unlocks the entire supplication.

Start with words that lift your soul:

> *"Alhamdulillāhi Rabbil-'ālamīn."*
> *"Subḥānaka Allāhumma wa biḥamdik."*
> *"Yā Ḥayy, Yā Qayyūm, Yā Raḥmān, Yā Raḥīm."*

Praise opens the heart.
Praise clears distraction.
Praise brings your soul into the correct posture before the One who hears every whisper of your need.

When you begin with ḥamd and thanā', you enter du'ā' the way the Prophets entered it — with reverence, awareness, and a heart already turned toward its Lord.

2. Send Ṣalawāt Upon the Prophet ﷺ

This is part of the Prophetic order:

1. Praise Allah
2. Send ṣalawāt upon the Prophet ﷺ
3. Then make your request

'Amr bin Malik Al-Janbi narrated that he heard Fadalah bin 'Ubaid saying:

"The Prophet ﷺ heard a man supplicating in his Salat but he did not send Salat upon the Prophet ﷺ, so the Prophet ﷺ said: 'This one has rushed.' Then he called him and said to him, or to someone other than him: 'When one of you performs Salat, then let him begin by expressing gratitude to Allah and praising Him. Then, let him send Salat upon the Prophet ﷺ, then let him supplicate after that, whatever he wishes.'" — *Jami' at-Tirmidhi 3477*

And at the end:

4. Close with ṣalawāt again

Scholars say:

> Allah *always* accepts the ṣalawāt.
> Allah is too generous to accept what surrounds your du'ā'
> and reject the du'ā' itself.

This is your acceptance envelope around your request.

3. Call Upon Allah Using His Beautiful Names —Asmā' al-Ḥusnā

Allah instructs us directly in the Qur'an:

> *"Allah has the Most Beautiful Names. So, call upon Him by them."*
>
> — Surat al-A'raf Q7:180

Du'ā' becomes more powerful when the Name you use matches the need in your heart. Every request has a Name that unlocks it:

- For protection, call upon Al-Ḥafīẓ and Al-Qawiyy.
- For provision, turn to Ar-Razzāq and Al-Wahhāb.
- For guidance, seek Al-Hādī.
- For forgiveness, plead with Al-Ghafūr and Ar-Raḥīm.
- For relief and gentle openings, invoke Al-Karīm and Al-Laṭīf.

And the most universal Name used by all Prophets:
Rabb / Rabbanā
This single Name carries within it the meanings of nurture, care, protection, guidance, sustenance, reform, and continual support. It is the Name of the One who raises you, guides you, and manages every detail of your life.

This is why nearly every major prophetic duʿāʾ begins with:

"Rabbī..."
"Rabbanā..."

It is a Name that fits every request—large or small—because it speaks directly to the One who has been taking care of you since before you were even aware of Him.

4. Raise Your Hands — Properly, With Awe

Raising your hand to people is humiliation.
Raising your hand to Allah is honour.

The Prophet ﷺ said:

> *"Allah is shy to reject the duʿāʾ of a servant who raises his hands to Him."*

Two valid sunnah positions:

1. Palms facing up toward the sky, looking at them.
2. Fingers raised upward while palms face yourself.

Both express humility and need.

5. Face the Qiblah — *When Possible*

Facing the Qiblah is not obligatory when making duʿāʾ, but it is a Sunnah that carries dignity and focus. The Prophet ﷺ would turn to the Qiblah during significant moments of supplication, such as on the Day of Badr and during the major duʿāʾ at ʿArafah.

ʿUmar ibn al-Khaṭṭāb رضي الله عنه describes the Prophet ﷺ on the day of Badr:

> *"The Prophet ﷺ faced the Qiblah, stretched out his hands, and began supplicating intensely..."*

Facing the Qiblah aligns the body with the heart. It signals intentionality, presence, and reverence. It reminds you that you are directing your request toward the Lord of the Kaʿbah, the One who commanded this direction and made it a symbol of unity and devotion.

When possible, turn your face toward the Qiblah. It gathers your concentration and places you in the posture of the Prophets and the righteous who prayed before you.

6. Seek Forgiveness Before Requesting

After praising Allah and sending ṣalawāt, let your first personal words be words of repentance. Begin with istighfār. Whisper:

> *"Astaghfirullāh"*
> "Yā Allah, forgive me."

Istighfār softens the heart and clears the spiritual pathway. Sin weighs a duʿāʾ down; repentance lifts it. The scholars explain that sins act as barriers, while sincere repentance removes those barriers, so your request rises unhindered.

Allah Himself highlights the power of istighfār in **Sūrat Nūḥ**, where Prophet Nūḥ عليه السلام tells his people:

"Ask forgiveness of your Lord;
indeed, He is Ever-Forgiving.
He will send rain to you in abundance,
and He will strengthen you with wealth and children..."

— Sūrat Nūḥ *Q71:10–12*

Istighfār is not only a cleansing— it is a source of provision, relief, openings, and answered prayers. Before asking for anything, cleanse the space between you and your Lord. A du'ā' that begins with forgiveness is a du'ā' that travels upward with ease.

7. Mention a Sincere Good Deed — *Use ONLY When Desperate*

This is a high-impact spiritual key.

This etiquette comes from the famous incident of the three men who were trapped in a cave. A huge boulder blocked the entrance, and each man called upon Allah by mentioning one sincere deed he had done purely for His sake. With every deed mentioned, the rock shifted a little, until Allah freed them completely.

This is not a tool to use casually.
It is a lifeline, reserved for the moments when the heart is truly desperate and there is no door left except the door of Allah.

Because of this, it is wise for a believer to quietly accumulate good deeds throughout life—unseen, unadvertised, unrecorded by anyone but Allah.

Think in terms of building a private portfolio of acts that are for His eyes alone.

A moment of hidden charity.
A night prayer no one witnessed.

An act of forgiveness you never publicised.
A kindness to someone who could never repay you.

These are the deeds you "store" for hardship, the deeds you can confidently present to Allah in a moment of crisis.

Cultivating this mindset shifts how you live each day.

You begin asking yourself:
What can I do today that is sincere enough to call upon later?
Which private act can I give to Allah that He can turn into relief for me when I need it most?

You stop performing for people and start investing in the unseen.

Every quiet, righteous act becomes a future opening, a door of mercy waiting for its appointed time.

Then, in the moment of deep need, you may say:

"Yā Allah, You know the deed I did secretly for Your sake.
If You accepted it from me, let it be a means of relief today."

Use this key sparingly and with sincerity.
Its power lies in purity—and in the fact that it is drawn only when the heart is in genuine need.

8. Present Your Weakness and Need —*The Way of the Prophets*

A powerful du'ā' is never made from a place of pride.
It is made from a place of truth — the truth that we are weak, limited, forgetful, and entirely dependent on Allah.

Every Prophet modelled this humility before making their request. Their du'ā's carried weight because they admitted their need.

Consider Ādam عليه السلام, whose words still echo through human history:

> *"Our Lord! We have wronged ourselves. If You do not forgive us and have mercy on us, we will certainly be losers."*
>
> — Surat al-A'rāf Q7:23

There is no self-defence in his plea — only honesty.

Zakariyyā عليه السلام expressed the fragility of age with dignity and humility:

> *"My Lord! Surely my bones have become brittle,*
> *and grey hair has spread across my head..."*
>
> — Surat Maryam Q19:4

Not a complaint — a recognition of his human limits before the One who has no limits.

Mūsā عليه السلام stood in the shade exhausted, hungry, and alone, and confessed:

> *"Rabbi innī limā anzalta ilayya min khayrin faqīr."*
> "My Lord, I am in desperate need of whatever good You send me."
>
> — Surat al-Qaṣaṣ Q28:24

This is not just a du'ā' — it is surrender wrapped in dependence.

Yūsuf عليه السلام, pressured with temptation and injustice, declared:

> *"If You do not turn their plot away from me, I will fall into it."*

He did not rely on his purity, strength, or willpower. He relied on Allah alone.

This is the Prophetic pattern:
acknowledge your weakness before you ask for strength,
admit your limits before you seek Allah's limitless help.

In your own du'ā', let it sound like this:
"Yā Allah, I am weak — strengthen me."
"Yā Allah, my heart is tired — revive it."
"Yā Allah, without You I cannot stand."
"Yā Rabb, if You do not help me, I cannot help myself."

Allah loves the heart that comes to Him broken, truthful, and leaning entirely upon Him. Because the one who admits their need is the one who is most ready to receive.

9. Ask for Your Request — Clearly, Boldly, With Certainty

Once you have praised Allah, sent ṣalawāt, expressed your weakness, and aligned your heart with humility, now you ask.

This is the moment when your need meets His generosity.

Do not hold back.
Ask for your dunya and your ākhirah.
Ask for clarity, guidance, healing, protection, rizq, marriage, children, success, relief, elevation — whatever your heart carries.

Ask big.
Nothing is too great for the One who created the heavens without effort.

The Prophet ﷺ taught us to repeat our du'ā' up to three times, especially when the matter is important.
Repetition shows eagerness, urgency, and sincerity.

It is not a lack of trust —
it is a sign of longing.

And when you ask, ask with certainty, never hesitation.
The Prophet ﷺ said:

"Call upon Allah while being certain of His response."

Speak with conviction:
"Yā Allah, grant me..."
"Yā Allah, open the doors of goodness for me..."
"Yā Allah, protect me from what I cannot see..."
"Yā Allah, provide for me and place barakah in it..."

Allah loves a servant who knows exactly what they need,
who articulates it clearly,
who believes deeply that Allah can bring it to life.

10. Lower Your Voice — But Speak from the Heart

Du'ā' is not a performance. It is an intimate conversation between you and the One who hears even the unspoken thoughts of your heart.

You do not need to raise your voice or force emotion.
Allah does not require loudness —
He requires sincerity.

The Qur'an instructs us to call upon Allah with humility and softness.

Your voice should be low, gentle, and respectful —
not shouted or strained.

The power of du'ā' is not in its volume,
but in its truthfulness.

Sometimes the most powerful du'ā' is a whisper.
Sometimes it is a tear.
Sometimes it is a sentence that only Allah can hear.

He hears the tremor in your voice.
He hears the quiet ache behind your words.
He hears the whisper of your soul before it becomes sound.

Lower your voice — and let your heart speak.

11. Have Positive Expectation — *Husn al-Dhann biLlāh*

A powerful du'ā' is built on certainty —
not uncertainty, not fear, not hesitation.

When you raise your hands, you are not speaking to a distant Lord, but to the One who calls Himself **al-Mujīb**, the One who responds.

The Prophet ﷺ said that Allah declares:

"I am as My servant thinks of Me."

This means your expectation shapes the experience of your du'ā'.

Do not think your du'ā' is:

- too small to matter
- too big to be granted
- too complicated for Allah's mercy

Nothing is beyond His ability, and nothing is beneath His care.

Think well of Him.
Believe that He hears you, that He sees you, that He understands the layers of your request even better than you do.

Expect the best — even if the answer arrives in a form different from what you imagined.

Sometimes Allah gives immediately.
Sometimes He withholds to protect you.
Sometimes He delays to elevate you.
And sometimes He reserves something far greater for the Hereafter.

A heart that assumes goodness from Allah,
will always find goodness with Him.

12. Repeat Your Duʿāʾ — *Especially When Your Heart Truly Wants Something*

Ibn Masʿūd رضي الله عنه reported that when the Prophet ﷺ made duʿāʾ, he would repeat it **three times**.

> "When the Prophet ﷺ supplicated, he would supplicate three times, and when he asked, he would ask three times."
> — Sunan Abi Dawud 1524

This repetition is not a lack of trust —
it is an expression of yearning.

It shows that the matter is close to the heart,
that it carries weight,
that it genuinely matters to you.

Repetition deepens sincerity.
It softens the heart.

It gathers your scattered emotions
and aligns them toward the same request.

Every time you repeat the du'ā',
it becomes more focused,
more honest,
more alive.

If there is something your heart aches for,
ask once —
then ask again —
then ask a third time.

Not mechanically,
but with presence.

Let each repetition carry more truth than the one before it.

Repetition is the language of longing,

and Allah responds to hearts that long for Him.

13. Close the Du'ā' With Ṣalawāt

A powerful du'ā' ends with dignity, gratitude, and honour.

After making your request, send ṣalawāt upon the Prophet ﷺ again.

This is not repetition for the sake of repetition;
it is the **Prophetic seal**.

The scholars explain that Allah always accepts praise of Him
and always accepts ṣalawāt upon His Messenger.

And Allah is too generous to accept what surrounds your du'ā' and reject what lies between.

By ending your du'ā' with the same reverence you began with, you wrap your request in a complete, balanced, and beautiful form — an envelope of acceptance.

14. Choose the Times When Du'ā' Is Most Likely Accepted

Du'ā' can be made at any moment, but the Prophet ﷺ highlighted certain times when the doors of acceptance open wider.

These are moments when the veil between you and Allah feels thinner, when the heart softens naturally, and when Allah's mercy descends in abundance.

Seek these times intentionally:

- **In the last third of the night** — when Allah calls His servants, asking who seeks His forgiveness and who needs His help.
- **Between the adhān and iqāmah** — a window of serenity where du'ā' is not rejected.
- **While fasting** — when the heart is humbled and the ego subdued.
- **Just before breaking the fast** — a moment loaded with sincerity and closeness.
- **In the final hour before Maghrib on Friday** — a time the Prophet ﷺ described as a special moment of acceptance.
- And **in sujūd** — the position in which a servant is closest to Allah — where du'ā' is most beloved.

And beyond these, the Sunnah highlights many other blessed moments:

- **During rainfall** — when mercy descends from the sky.

- **At the end of obligatory prayers** — after the final tashahhud and before salām.
- **On the Day of 'Arafah** — the greatest day of du'ā' in the year.
- **After wuḍū'** — when purity softens and prepares the heart.
- **When drinking Zamzam water** — accompanied by sincere intention.
- **During calamity or hardship** — when the heart breaks open before Allah.
- **During travel** — when the prayer of a traveller is readily accepted.
- **When a Muslim prays for their brother or sister in their absence** — a du'ā' the angels echo back with *"Āmīn, and for you the same."*
- **The du'ā' of parents for their children** — one of the most powerful prayers on earth.
- **In the first ten days of Dhul-Hijjah** — days filled with divine light and elevation.
- **And on Laylat al-Qadr** — the Night of Decree — the greatest night of the entire year.

When you combine proper etiquette with the right timing, you multiply the chances of acceptance.

These moments are gifts — touchpoints of mercy scattered throughout the week and year.

Seek them,
stand in them,
and let your heart pour out its need.

15. End With Surrender

After you have asked,
poured out your heart,
repeated your need,
and wrapped your du'ā' in ṣalawāt,
there remains one final step — **surrender**.

True *tawakkul* begins where your request ends.

Surrender is not giving up.
It is handing the outcome to the One who sees what you cannot,
who knows what you never will,
and who protects you even from the things you desperately want.

It is the recognition that His wisdom is perfect
and your vision is limited.

Let your du'ā' close with words like:
"Yā Allah, choose what is best for me."
"If this matter is khayr, bring it with ease; and if it is not, turn my heart and my path away from it."
"Yā Rabb, I trust Your wisdom over my desire."

Surrender transforms du'ā' from a transaction into a relationship.
It frees you from anxiety,
softens the heart,
and anchors you in the certainty that whatever Allah chooses
will always be better than anything you could have chosen for yourself.

11.3 — The Prophet's Morning Du'ā' Blueprint

Here are the core morning supplications the Prophet ﷺ used to make regularly:

1. Du'ā' for Pardon and Well-being

"Allahumma innee as-alukal-'afwa wal'afiyah, fid-dunya wal-akhirah,"
O Allah, I ask You for pardon and well-being in this life and the next.

2. Du'ā' for the Good of the Day

Rabbi as'aluka khayra mā fī hādha-l-yawmi wa khayra mā ba'dah,
"My Lord, I ask You for the good that is in this day and the good that follows it,"

3. Protection from the Evil of the Day

wa a'ūdhu bika min sharri mā fī hādha-l-yawmi wa sharri mā ba'dah.
"and I seek Your protection from the evil that is in this day and from the evil that follows it. "

4. Protection From Laziness & Weakness

Rabbi a'ūdhu bika mina-l-kasali wa sū'i-l-kibar,

"My Lord, I seek Your protection from laziness and the misery of old age."

5. Protection From Fire & the Grave

Rabbi a'ūdhu bika min 'adhābin fi-n-nāri wa 'adhābin fi-l-qabr.

"My Lord, I seek Your protection from the torment of the Hell-fire and the punishment of the grave."

The Prophet ﷺ never began a day without these. These du'ā's shape the emotional, spiritual, and physical direction of your day.

Aṣbaḥnā wa aṣbaḥa-l-mulku li-llāh, wa-l-ḥamdu li-llāh,
lā ilāha illa-llāhu waḥdahū lā sharīka lah,
lahu-l-mulku wa lahu-l-ḥamd,
wa huwa ʿalā kulli shay'in Qadīr.

Rabbi as'aluka khayra mā fī hādha-l-yawmi
wa khayra mā baʿdah,
wa aʿūdhu bika min sharri mā fī hādha-l-yawmi
wa sharri mā baʿdah.

Rabbi aʿūdhu bika mina-l-kasal wa sū'i-l-kibar.
Rabbi aʿūdhu bika min ʿadhābin fi-n-nār
wa ʿadhābin fi-l-qabr.

We have entered the morning,
and at this very time the whole kingdom belongs to Allah.
All praise is due to Allah.
There is no god worthy of worship except Allah, the One;
He has no partner with Him.
The entire kingdom belongs solely to Him,
to Him is all praise due,
and He is All-Powerful over everything.

My Lord, I ask You for the good that is in this day
and the good that follows it.
And I seek Your protection from the evil that is in this day
and from the evil that follows it.
My Lord, I seek Your protection from laziness
and the misery of old age.
My Lord, I seek Your protection
from the torment of the Hell-fire
and the punishment of the grave.

11.4 — The Four Types of Morning Du'ā'

Not every morning feels the same, and not every heart arrives with the same capacity. Some days you have time. Some days you don't. Some days your heart is raw and open; other days it needs gentle coaxing.

Your du'ā' should flex with your state.

Choose the type that fits your morning or rotate between them throughout the week. What matters is consistency, sincerity, and presence.

Type 1 — The 60-Second, Heart-Press Du'ā'

For mornings on the move.
A quick but genuine connection that anchors your day.

Raise your hands.
Say three sincere lines.
Let your chest speak, even if your mind is tired.

In one minute, you can align your heart with Allah and start the day centred, calm, and spiritually awake.

Type 2 — The 3-Part Structured Du'ā' (5 minutes)

A short, balanced formula that never fails:

1. **Praise** — recognise who Allah is.
2. **Gratitude** — acknowledge His blessings.
3. **Request** — ask clearly for what you need today.

Five minutes.
Focused, grounded, complete.

Type 3 — The Qur'ānic Du'ā' Mode

When you want safety, clarity, and guaranteed spiritual depth, use the du'ā's Allah Himself taught us.

Examples:

1. ***"Rabbi zidnī 'ilmā."***

"My Lord, increase me in knowledge."

— Surah Tāhā Q20:114

The only du'ā' in the Qur'ān where Allah directly commands the Prophet ﷺ to ask for more of something —
and that "something" is **knowledge**.

2. **"Rabbana ātina fid-dunyā ḥasanah..."**

"Our Lord, give us good in this world and good in the Hereafter, and protect us from the punishment of the Fire."

— Surah Al-Baqarah Q2:201

A comprehensive du'ā' that gathers dunya + ākhirah in one breath.

3. ***"Rabbi inni limā anzalta ilayya min khayrin faqīr."***

"My Lord, I am in desperate need of whatever good You send down to me."

— Surah Al-Qasas 28:24

The du'ā' of Mūsā عليه السلام when exhausted, alone, and helpless —
a prayer of total surrender and dependence.

4. ***"Rabbishraḥ lī ṣadrī Wa yassir li 'amri"***

"My Lord, expand my chest and ease my task for me."

— Surah Tāhā Q20:25–26

A Prophetic du'ā' for confidence, clarity, and ease before any challenge.

5. ***"Rabbana la tuzigh quloobana ba'da idh hadaitana wa hab lana milladunka rahmah innaka antal Wahhab"***

"Our Lord, do not let our hearts deviate after You have guided us, and grant us mercy from Yourself — You are the Giver of Gifts."

— Surah Āl 'Imrān Q3:8

A du'ā' for spiritual stability, protection, and divine mercy.

These are timeless, comprehensive, tested by the Prophets, and preserved in the Qur'an.
If you don't know what to say, Qur'ānic du'ā' is always the safest and most powerful path.

Safe. Powerful. Complete.

Type 4 — The Deep Du'ā' (10–15 minutes)

This is your spiritual reset.
A full, unfiltered conversation with Allah — the kind that unclutters the heart and steadies the soul.

You speak.
You pause.
You breathe.
You confess.
You ask.
You surrender.

This du'ā' is not rushed. It is not formulaic. It is the moment where everything you've been carrying finally finds a place to land.

These four types give you flexibility, structure, and sustainability.
Some days you whisper.
Some days you speak.
Some days you pour.

But every day — you turn back to Allah.

11.5 — What to Ask for in the Morning (Dunya + Ākhirah)

Morning du'ā' sets the tone for your entire day.
What you ask for at dawn shapes your heart, your character, your rizq, your decisions, and your destiny.

And nothing is too small to bring to Allah.
Nothing is too big.
Your Lord is **Al-Karīm** — the Most Generous.

Here is what your heart should reach for each morning.

Ask for Your Religion

Start with what matters most:

Ask Allah for sincerity that never wavers.
For consistency that survives your moods.
For khushū' that melts hardness from your heart.
For the ability to pray on time with presence.
For Qur'ān that penetrates your chest instead of sitting on your tongue.
For a tongue busy with dhikr, not distraction.

Ask to be a servant who remembers Him before remembering the world.

Ask for Your Character

Your character determines the quality of your relationships, your peace, and your ākhirah.

Ask for patience that doesn't collapse under pressure.
For gentleness that softens conflict.
For emotional regulation that lifts you above impulses.
For the removal of jealousy and envy that corrupt the soul.
For strength in moments of difficulty.
For wisdom in speech — words that heal, not harm.

Good character is a daily gift from Allah.

Ask for Your Life

This is your dunya — the vessel you're travelling in.

Ask for halal rizq that nourishes without burdening you.
For ease in your tasks and projects.
For barakah in your time, your energy, your work.
For protection from harm — seen and unseen, human and jinn.
For solutions to problems before they overwhelm you.
For guidance in decisions that will shape the rest of your life.

Everything becomes easier when Allah supports your day.

Ask for Your Future

Because every morning is a step toward the hereafter.

Ask for a good ending.
For a grave that is peaceful, spacious, and filled with light.
For ease on the Day of Judgment.
For the ability to meet Allah with a sound, purified heart — a heart that loved Him, trusted Him, and returned to Him sincerely.

This is the ultimate success.

Ask for Your Family

Those closest to you deserve your duʿāʾ just as much as you do.

Ask for their protection — physically, emotionally, and spiritually.
For guidance that keeps them near Allah.
For peace in your home.
For unity between hearts.
For healing from what they carry, and healing from what you do not see.

The best gift you can give your family is a sincere duʿāʾ made in their absence.

There is **no small request** in duʿāʾ.
There is **no dream too large** for the One who says *"Be,"* and it is.
Your Lord is **Al-Karīm** —
so ask Him like you know His generosity.

Ask for Your Parents

Whether they are alive or returned to Allah,
your parents are among the greatest recipients of your duʿāʾ.

Ask Allah to have mercy on them.
To forgive their mistakes.
To expand their provision.
To soften their hearts and keep them upon guidance.

Ask for their health, their comfort, their happiness,
and for your own heart to honour them with gentleness and patience.

If they have passed away,
ask Allah to fill their graves with light,
to raise their ranks in the highest gardens,
and to bless them with continuous reward through your deeds.

A child's sincere du'ā'
is one of the most powerful gifts a parent can receive.

Ask for the Ummah

Your du'ā' carries weight beyond your own life.
Every believer is part of your spiritual family — those living now, those who came before, and those who will come after.

Ask Allah to heal the Ummah.
To lift oppression wherever it exists.
To restore dignity, justice, and unity.
To protect the weak, the forgotten, and the displaced.
To guide our youth, strengthen our scholars, and bless every sincere effort done for His sake.

Ask Allah to give victory to truth, to revive faith in the hearts,
and to make you a source of light within this Ummah —
even in the smallest ways.

When you pray for the Ummah,
the angels pray for you.

Ask for Those Who Have Passed Away

Death does not silence love —
it simply redirects it toward du'ā'.

Ask Allah to forgive their sins
and multiply their good deeds.
To make their graves spacious and full of peace.
To let light reach them when they are alone.
To allow your charity, your Qur'ān, and your kindness
to reach them as ongoing reward.

Ask Allah to reunite you with them in Jannah —
in a place where no one will part again.

Your du'ā' is a rope of mercy
extended to those who can no longer act for themselves.
Every time you remember them,
Allah remembers you.

11.6 — Du'ā' Templates for Different Seasons of Life

Life unfolds in seasons. Each season carries its own challenges, hopes, fears, and openings. The Qur'an and Sunnah give us du'ā's for every one of these moments—timeless, comprehensive, and divinely crafted.

Below are templates based on Qur'anic prayers and authentic ahādīth, adapted for each circumstance, with clear sourcing.
Use them as they are, or build your own upon them.

For the Parent

Qur'anic du'ā' for family mercy and righteousness:

"Rabbana hab lanā min azwājinā wa dhurriyyātinā qurrata a'yun, waj'alnā lil-muttaqīna imāmā."
"Our Lord, grant us from our spouses and children comfort to our eyes, and

make us leaders for the righteous."

— Qur'an 25:74

This encompasses mercy, calm, guidance, and righteous offspring.

For the Student

A Qur'anic du'ā' for knowledge and clarity:

> ***"Rabbi zidnī 'ilmā."***
> "My Lord, increase me in knowledge."
>
> — Qur'an 20:114

And a du'ā' for ease in learning and performing tasks:

> ***"Rabbi yassir wa lā tu'assir, wa tammim bil-khayr."***
> "My Lord, make it easy and do not make it difficult, and complete it with goodness."

For the Professional

The Prophet ﷺ taught this powerful du'ā' for clarity and guidance:

"Allāhumma inni as'aluka 'ilman nāfi'ā, wa rizqan ṭayyibā, wa 'amalan mutaqabbalā."
"O Allah, I ask You for beneficial knowledge, pure sustenance, and accepted deeds."

— Sunan Ibn Mājah

This single du'ā' covers focus, clarity, and halal success.

For the Entrepreneur

A du'ā' seeking correct decisions and divine protection:

"Rabbi ishraḥ lī ṣadrī, wa yassir lī amrī."
"My Lord, expand my chest for me and make my affairs easy."
— Qur'an 20:25–26

And the du'ā' of guidance in choices:

"Allāhumma khir lī wakhtar lī"
"O Allah, make it good for me and choose for me."

Aishah narrated from Abu Bakr As-Siddiq,: ﵁

that whenever the Prophet ﷺ wanted to do a matter, he would say:
"O Allah, make it good for me and choose for me."
— Jami'at-Tirmidhi 3516

For the One Struggling or Overwhelmed

The du'ā' of Prophet Yūnus عليه السلام in distress:

> ***"Lā ilāha illā Anta, subḥānaka innī kuntu minaz-zālimīn."***
> "There is no god but You; glory be to You; truly I was among the wrongdoers."
> — Qur'an 21:87

The Prophet ﷺ said:
"No one supplicates with this du'ā' except that Allah removes his distress."
— Sunan al-Tirmidhī 3505

For the Sick One

A direct Prophetic du'ā' for healing:

> ***"Azhibil ba'sa Robban-naasi washfi antash-shaafi laa shifaa-a illa shifaa-uka shifaa-an laa yughaadiru saqama."***
> "O Allah, Lord of mankind, remove the harm and heal, for You are the Healer; there is no healing except Yours."
> — Sahih Bukhari & Muslim

For the One Seeking Marriage

A Qur'anic du'ā' for righteous companionship:

> ***"Rabbana hab lanā min ladunka zawjan ṣāliḥā."*** *(adapted structurally)*

Meaning derived from Qur'an 66:11 & 25:74 (righteous spouses as a gift).

And also:

> ***"Rabbi inni limā anzalta ilayya min khayrin faqīr."***
> "My Lord, I am in desperate need of whatever good You send me."
> *— Qur'an 28:24*

Scholars mention this includes seeking righteous companionship.

For the One Seeking Rizq

Direct Qur'anic and Prophetic sources:

> ***"Rabbi inni limā anzalta ilayya min khayrin faqīr."***
> "I am in desperate need of the good You send."
> — Qur'an 28:24

And the Prophet ﷺ taught:

"Allāhumma ikfinī biḥalālika 'an ḥarāmik, wa aghninī bi faḍlika 'amman siwāk."

"O Allah, suffice me with what You made halal, keep me from what You made haram, and enrich me with Your bounty over all others."

— Sunan al-Tirmidhī

For the One Seeking Inner Peace

A Qur'anic du'ā' for tranquillity of heart:

"Rabbish raḥ lī ṣadrī."

"My Lord, expand my chest."

— Qur'an 20:25

And the du'ā' from the Sunnah:

"Allāhumma inni as'aluka nafsan muṭma'innah."

"O Allah, grant me a soul that is content and tranquil."

— Derived from Qur'an 89:27–30 and authenticated in meaning through du'ā' of well-being

These templates help build your du'ā' language

The more Qur'anic and Prophetic your du'ā' becomes,
the more powerful, protected, and spiritually anchored it is.

You are not just asking from your own words—
you are asking through the words Allah and His Messenger ﷺ taught for every season of life.

11.7 — The Barakah of Specificity

The Prophet ﷺ did not make vague or generic du'ā'.
His supplications were clear, detailed, intentional, and deeply personal. This is because **specific du'ā' reflects a heart that knows what it needs and trusts that Allah can deliver it**.

Specificity reveals four qualities:

Clarity — you understand your own state.
Intention — you know what direction you want Allah to guide you.
Trust — you believe Allah can shape the details of your life.
Sincerity — you are not performing; you are genuinely asking.

Generic du'ā' produces generic change.
Specific du'ā' produces specific transformation.

For example, instead of saying:

"Yā Allah, make my day good,"
which is beautiful but broad, try saying:

"Yā Allah, grant me ease in my tasks, barakah in my time, gentleness in my speech, protection from unnecessary stress, and clarity in every decision I make today."

The difference is immediate.
One du'ā' is a blanket hope; the other is a roadmap.

When you are specific, you involve Allah in the details of your life — and that is where barakah lives.

11.8 — The Du'ā' Journal — Optional but Incredibly Powerful

A du'ā' journal is not about writing beautifully. It is about witnessing your relationship with Allah unfold over time. Keeping a small morning du'ā' journal turns your supplication into a lived, traceable journey.

Each morning, write down just three lines:

one gratitude,

> *Yā Allah, thank You for waking me up today and giving me another chance to begin again.*

one request,

> *Yā Allah, grant me clarity in my work today and protect my heart from anxiety.*

one surrender.

> *Yā Allah, whatever You choose for me today, I trust that it is better than what I would choose for myself.*

These lines do not need to be long.
They do not need to sound perfect.
They only need to be honest.

It takes less than a minute, but the spiritual impact accumulates over months.

Slowly, you begin to see patterns—how Allah removed things that were harming you, how He gave you what you were not brave enough to ask for, how He protected you from what you thought you wanted, and how He replaced your losses with something better.

Your journal becomes a map of answered prayers, delayed prayers, redirected prayers, and prayers that were transformed into protection or barakah.

Du'ā' is not just words; it is an ongoing relationship.
A journal helps you see how Allah has been holding you, guiding you, and responding to you long before you realised it.

11.9 — What to Do When Du'ā' Feels Unanswered

Every believer reaches a moment where the heart whispers,
"Why hasn't it happened yet?"

Understanding the nature of du'ā' brings calm to that moment. Du'ā' is never ignored, never lost, never wasted. Allah responds in ways the heart sometimes sees only in hindsight.

Here is how to anchor yourself when your du'ā' feels unanswered.

1. It *was* answered — but differently.

Not every response looks like the thing you requested.

Sometimes Allah answers through **protection**—keeping a harm away you never even knew was coming.
Sometimes He answers through **delay**—giving you what you asked for at the exact moment it will benefit you most.
Sometimes He answers through **redirection**—turning you away from something that would have broken you.

Different is not denial.
Different is mercy in disguise.

2. Allah is preparing you.

Gifts often require capacity.
Sometimes the heart needs to stretch before it can carry what you are

asking for.
Sometimes your character, patience, or tawakkul needs to be strengthened first.

When Allah delays, He is often preparing the receiver before granting the request.
The wait is part of the gift.

3. Allah loves your voice.

There are moments when the blessing is delayed because your du'ā' itself is beloved to Allah.

Your voice in the early morning.
Your tears in sujūd.
Your whisper before iftar.
Your repeated return to Him.

Some supplications are prolonged because the state you enter while making them is more beloved to Allah than the thing you are asking for.

4. Keep asking — because nothing is ever wasted.

The Prophet ﷺ said:

"Du'ā' benefits what has descended (i.e., calamities that have occurred) and what has not yet descended (i.e., calamities that have not yet occurred). O servants of Allāh, cling to du'ā'."

— Tabarani

Your du'ā' pushes away hardship before it arrives.
Your du'ā' softens trials already unfolding.
Your du'ā' builds goodness you will meet in this life and the next.

Keep asking.
Keep returning.
Du'ā' is never lost.

11.10 — Troubleshooting

Even with the best intentions, du'ā' can sometimes feel confusing, awkward, or overwhelming. These are normal human experiences, not spiritual failures. Here is how to navigate them with ease and clarity.

"I don't know what to say."

Say *anything* honest.
There is no script. There is no "correct" wording.
You are speaking to the One who already knows what is in your heart before you form the sentence.

Honesty is richer than eloquence.

"I feel awkward raising my hands."

Then make du'ā' quietly.
Raising the hands is Sunnah, not a requirement.
There is no awkwardness with the One who created you, shaped you, and knows your insecurities better than you do.

Come as you are. He already sees you.

"I'm inconsistent."

Attach du'ā' to the anchors of your day:

- after Fajr

- after Duḥā
- before leaving home
- before starting work
- before sleep

Consistency grows from routines, not from willpower.
Tie your du'ā' to something that already happens, and your heart will naturally show up.

"I'm overwhelmed."

Go back to Qur'ānic du'ā's.
They are short.
They are powerful.
They are complete.
And they are guaranteed to be blessed because Allah Himself taught them.

When your mind is full, let the Qur'an speak for you.

Troubles are normal.
Returning to Allah despite them — that is worship.

Du'ā' transforms the morning
because it transforms the *heart*.

It turns your routines into worship,
your tasks into ibādah,
your stress into surrender,
your fear into trust,
your loneliness into connection.

A person who starts the day with du'ā'
walks through life with a shield.

Du'ā' is not just an act — it is a posture.
It is the believer standing with dignity before the Lord of Power, asking with certainty and trust.

And while every sincere supplication is heard, there are Qur'anic du'ā's that Allah Himself commands the believer to say. Not one. Several.

Allah teaches His servants *what to ask for* — and then commands them to speak it.

For example:

1. Qulillahumma Mālika-l-Mulk...
"Say: O Allah, Owner of all sovereignty..."
— Surah Āl-'Imrān Q3:26
Theme: Power, authority, honour, provision
Use when: You feel small before big outcomes.

2. Qul Rabba-ghfir warḥam wa anta khayru-r-rāḥimīn

"Say: My Lord, forgive and have mercy; You are the best of the merciful."
— Surah Al-Mu'minūn Q23:118
Theme: Forgiveness & mercy
Use when: You need cleansing, not just relief.

3. Qul Rabbi zidnī 'ilmā
"Say: My Lord, increase me in knowledge."
— Surah Ṭā-Hā 20:114
Theme: Growth in beneficial knowledge
Use when: You're learning, building, seeking clarity.

4. Qul Rabbi aʿūdhu bika min hamazāti-sh-shayāṭīn
"Say: My Lord, I seek refuge in You from the whispers of devils."
— Surah Al-Mu'minūn 23:97

Theme: Protection from inner and outer attacks
Use when: Your mind feels under siege.

5. Qul Rabbi anzilnī munzalan mubārakā
"Say: My Lord, grant me a blessed landing place."
— Surah Al-Mu'minūn 23:29

Theme: Barakah in transitions
Use when: Starting a new phase, move, project, or chapter.

6. Qul Rabbi adkhilnī mudkhala ṣidqin wa akhrijnī mukhraja ṣidqin...
"Say: My Lord, admit me with truth and let me exit with truth..."
— Surah Al-Isrā' 17:80

Theme: Integrity in beginnings and endings
Use when: Facing major decisions or changes.

7. Qul ḥasbiyallāhu lā ilāha illā Huwa...
"Say: Allah is sufficient for me. There is no deity but Him..."
— Surah At-Tawbah 9:129

Theme: Tawakkul (total reliance)
Use when: You've done all you can — now you hand it over.

8. Qul aʿūdhu birabbi-l-falaq
"Say: I seek refuge in the Lord of the daybreak..."
— Surah Al-Falaq 113:1

Theme: Protection from external harm
Use when: You fear what you can't see coming.

9. Qul aʿūdhu birabbi-n-nās
"Say: I seek refuge in the Lord of mankind..."
— Surah An-Nās 114:1

Theme: Protection from internal whispers
Use when: The battle is inside your chest.

These are du'ā's Allah did not merely record — He commanded.

But among these commanded supplications, there is one āyah that carries a unique morning power:

A declaration that reorders your mindset, anchors your heart, and aligns your entire day with Allah's control over outcomes.

Before we move to the final habit of this system, we will pause for a deep dive.

A master-dua.
A sovereignty declaration.
A morning ritual that has changed the lives of countless Muslims — and can transform yours.

This is the dua that resets your entire day.

CHAPTER 12

The Dua That Changes Your Day

Āl-'Imrān 3:26 — The Morning Sovereignty Ritual

Some āyāt of the Qur'an are recited.
Others are lived.

And then there are a select few where Allah explicitly commands the believer to *say* — deliberately, consciously, with a heart anchored in His power.

Āl-'Imrān 3:26 is one of those āyāt.

It is a declaration, not merely a dua.
A **reorientation of the heart**.
A **confession of truth**.
A **dismantling of false reliance**.

This is an āyah that teaches the soul — every single time — where power actually lives.

When recited after Fajr with understanding, this āyah does not just "start your day well."
It **reorders your expectations**,
restructures your reliance,
and **repositions your heart** in relation to Allah.

Most people wake up and step into their day carrying
uncertainty,
pressure,

delay,
fear,
or invisible emotional load.

This āyah meets you in that moment and lifts you into a completely different psychological and spiritual state. And that is why it produces results that feel — to the one who lives with it — unmistakably real.

The āyah.

قُلِ ٱللَّهُمَّ مَٰلِكَ ٱلْمُلْكِ تُؤْتِى ٱلْمُلْكَ مَن تَشَآءُ وَتَنزِعُ ٱلْمُلْكَ مِمَّن تَشَآءُ
وَتُعِزُّ مَن تَشَآءُ وَتُذِلُّ مَن تَشَآءُ ۖ بِيَدِكَ ٱلْخَيْرُ ۖ إِنَّكَ عَلَىٰ كُلِّ شَىْءٍ قَدِيرٌ ٢٦

"Say, ˹O Prophet,˺
'O Allah! Lord over all authorities!
You give authority to whoever You please
and remove it from who You please.
You honour whoever You please
and disgrace who You please —
all good is in Your Hands.
Surely You ˹alone˺ are Most Capable of everything.'"

A short āyah. But it points your heart to the One who controls all power, decree, generosity, and the management of every affair — including yours.

Allah does not merely record this āyah. He begins it with a command:

"Say."

This matters. Because Allah is not only informing you of His sovereignty — He is **establishing theological clarity before emotion flows**.

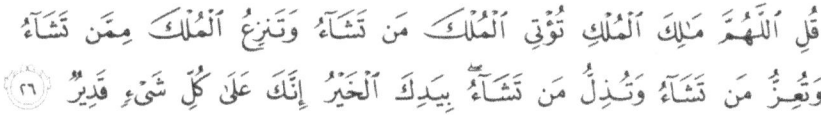

Āl-ʿImrān 3:26 anchors the heart in *who Allah is*
before the believer expresses *what they feel.*

Before need spills into words.
Before urgency rises.
Before fear, hope, desperation, or longing pour out in duʿāʾ.

Not to restrain emotion —
but to allow it to flow from a place of **clarity, not confusion**
from recognition, not assumption.
from certainty, not misdirected hope.

This clarity becomes an **anchor**.

An anchor that:

- steadies the heart while it pleads,
- grounds desperation in tawḥīd,
- prevents reliance from drifting toward creation,
- allows emotion to pour out without losing direction.

The believer does not ask *less* intensely.

They ask **more truthfully** —
knowing exactly Who hears,
Who owns outcomes,
and Who is capable of all things.

This is not a formula for how to make duʿāʾ.
It is a foundation for **knowing Who you are speaking to**.

When recited with understanding — particularly at the start of the day, it becomes one of the most powerful ways to enter the morning anchored in truth.

Why This Āyah Belongs in the Morning

The early morning is not random.

After Fajr:

- the heart is softer
- the mind is quieter
- the soul is more receptive
- distractions have not yet taken control

This is the moment before the world speaks to you. If you do not anchor your heart here, the world will anchor it for you —
to fear,
to people,
to outcomes,
to delays,
to comparison,
to pressure.

This ayah is not recited to feel inspired.
It is recited to establish reality.

Before emails.
Before responsibilities.
Before uncertainty.
Before demands.

You speak first —
and you speak truth.

A Line-by-Line Reorientation of the Heart

"O Allah! Lord over all authorities!

This is where you position yourself correctly.

You are not speaking to circumstances.
You are not speaking to people.
You are not speaking to systems.

You are speaking to:
The Owner of outcomes
The Owner of doors opening and closing
The Owner of opportunities
The Owner of provision
The Owner of honour
The Owner of every "yes," "no," and "not yet"

Nothing you will face today exists outside His ownership.

This kills dependence on people.
It ends panic.
It resets the heart to reality:
Allah owns everything you need today.

"You give authority to whoever You please ..."

This is not limited to rulers.

Allah gives:
Jobs
Promotions
Wealth
Clarity
Confidence
Influence
Stability

Companionship
Breakthroughs

Whatever you consider "a win" in this world — Allah gives it.

If you are waiting for something today —
it is not waiting on people.
It is waiting on Allah's will.

This line re-routes the believer away from chasing creation.

"… and remove it from who You please;"

Nothing you possess is permanent.
No position.
No income.
No status.
No comfort.

Allah can remove something:

- while you are alive
- or by removing *you* from it entirely

This is not meant to frighten you.
It is meant to **free you from attachment**.

You are reminded each morning:
Hold blessings lightly.
Anchor yourself in Allah tightly.

"You honour whoever You please…"

Honour is not wealth.
Honour is not status.
Honour is not visibility.

Allah can honour a person who owns nothing
and strip honour from one who owns everything.

Honour comes from:

- contentment
- self-respect
- independence from people
- dignity of faith
- closeness to Allah

This line restores **inner dignity**.

"And disgrace who You please..."

If Allah withdraws honour, no platform can restore it.
If Allah grants honour, no human can remove it.

This line teaches:

- emotional independence
- freedom from people's approval
- security that does not fluctuate

Your value is settled **above**, not negotiated below.

"—all good is in Your Hands ..."

All khayr — without exception.

Every solution
Every opening
Every idea
Every connection
Every source of rizq
Every healing
Every breakthrough

If Allah wills good for you, it reaches you.
If He withholds, it was not good for you — yet.

This line is pure serenity.

"Surely You ˹alone˺ are Most Capable of everything."

This is certainty.

Allah can:
Turn Weakness into Strength
Turn Fear into Courage
Turn Pressure into Relief
Turn Delay into Timing
Turn Closed Doors into New Paths
Turn "Impossible" into "Done"

This closes the āyah with absolute trust.

The Morning Recitation Method — *As Lived, Not Theorised*

To activate this dua, recite it **with presence**.

Step 1 — Sit in a calm state after Fajr

Disconnect from noise.
Let your breath settle.

Step 2 — Recite the āyah slowly

Not rushed.
Not memorised on autopilot.

Step 3 — Repeat it 3×

- First time: your tongue says it
- Second time: your mind understands it
- Third time: your heart absorbs it

Repetition is not ritual — it is *installation.*

Step 4 — Immediately follow with your personal dua

Now that your heart is aligned with Allah's sovereignty, ask Him for what you truly need.

You can speak in any language.

This is the moment your dua is strongest.

What to Ask for After This Dua

Ask with dignity.
Ask with confidence.
Ask for provision
Ask for children
Ask for marriage
Ask for relief
Ask for healing
Ask for direction

Ask for strength
Ask, knowing that you're speaking to the One who can make it happen.

Some examples:

If you need provision:
"Ya Allah, expand my halal rizq today."
If you feel overwhelmed:
"Ya Allah, lift this heaviness from my heart."
If you need clarity:
"Ya Allah, guide my decisions today."
If you're seeking companionship:
"Ya Allah, send me a spouse who brings me closer to You."
If you're in a waiting season:
"Ya Allah, open the door that is best for me."
If you need strength:
"Ya Allah, make me strong, calm, and firm."

This is a relationship, not a script.

Morning Reflection Prompts

This dua becomes even more powerful when paired with a few self-checks:

- What blessing today am I trusting too much in people for?
- What fear do I need to hand over to Allah?
- Which outcome do I keep trying to control?
- Where do I need honour from Allah, not others?
- What khayr am I overlooking in my current situation?

Reflection internalises the meaning.

Guided Closing Dua

Read this slowly after your personal dua:

"O Allah, Owner of all dominion, open for me the doors You know I need. Place honour in my life, clarity in my heart, and barakah in my provision. Protect me from harm. Make my day light, my decisions guided, and my heart anchored in trust. You are capable of all things."

Ameen.

Why This Ritual Elevates Your Barakah Morning

The Barakah Morning is built on habits that create spiritual alignment early in the day. This dua integrates seamlessly by:

Grounding Your Heart
Amplifying Your Duʿāʾ Habit
Reinforcing Tawakkul
Stabilising Your Emotions
Guiding Your Mindset
Unlocking Barakah Pathways

It ensures you don't just start the day "awake" — you start the day **aligned**.

Aligned with Allah's power.
Aligned with His decree.
Aligned with the truth that everything you seek is in His Hand.

That alignment is what transforms an ordinary morning into a barakah-filled one.

CHAPTER 13

Habit 9 — Practice Morning Ṣadaqah

The Habit That Unlocks Provision, Protection, and Ease

There is a secret that spiritually successful Muslims know:
If you want barakah in your day, give at the start of it.

Even a small act — a pound, a smile, a shared link, a helpful message — carries the weight of mountains when done early, quietly, and consistently.

The Prophet ﷺ said:

> *"Charity extinguishes sins like water extinguishes fire."*
>
> — Tirmidhī

And another narration:

> *"Sadaqah does not decrease wealth."*
>
> — Muslim

Morning ṣadaqah is not simply "being generous."
It is a *strategy* — a spiritual investment that clears your path, opens doors, protects you from harm, and draws divine help into your day.

13.1 — Why Morning Sadaqah?

Giving in the morning is not just charity — it is strategy.

It shapes your heart, protects your day, and invites a level of barakah that nothing else can replicate.

Here is why morning ṣadaqah carries such weight.

1. It sets the tone for your entire day.

When your first act of the day is giving, your heart learns to operate from generosity, not scarcity.

You begin your morning as someone who contributes, not someone who fears loss.

That single act shifts your mindset for the hours ahead.

2. It protects you from unseen harms.

The Prophet ﷺ described ṣadaqah as **a shield**.
Just as a physical shield protects from danger, charity protects from unseen harm, misfortune, and spiritual disturbance.

You step into the day covered by a divine protection you cannot manufacture alone.

3. It invites barakah into your work, business, and decisions.

People who give early often notice something remarkable: their day **"flows."**

Meetings go smoother, conversations open doors, tasks feel lighter, clarity arrives unexpectedly, and help appears from places they never anticipated.

Morning ṣadaqah places barakah at the front of your day so that everything that follows carries its fragrance.

4. It purifies your rizq.

Every income has hidden imperfections — things you overlooked, shortcuts you didn't mean to take, moments of haste, distractions that seeped into your intention.

Ṣadaqah cleans your earnings the way water cleans the hands.

Even the smallest amount purifies what you earn and what you hope to earn.

5. It softens the heart.

Giving softens hardness, dissolves ego, and expands compassion.

A heart that gives in the morning becomes a heart that is lighter, calmer, and more open for the rest of the day.

6. It anchors your day in gratitude.

You give because Allah gave you. Ṣadaqah is a quiet acknowledgment that everything in your hands came from His generosity first.

Beginning the day with gratitude invites more to be grateful for.

Morning ṣadaqah is small in action but massive in impact.

It changes how you feel,
how you think,
how you work,
and how Allah opens your day before you.

13.2 — *The Myth of "I Need Money to Give"*

Many people hold back from charity because they think giving requires money.

But in Islam, **ṣadaqah is not limited to money**.
It is far broader, far more accessible, and woven into every moment of your day.

The Prophet ﷺ said:

> *"Every act of goodness is charity."*
> — Al-Bukhari

This means your morning ṣadaqah can take countless forms:
A sincere smile.
A supportive message to someone having a hard day.
A reminder that benefits the heart.
Sharing knowledge online.
Helping someone complete a task.
Making du'ā' privately for a friend.
Removing something harmful from someone's path.
Even **staying silent when you feel angry** is charity — because you protected others from your words.

You never run out of opportunities for ṣadaqah.
As long as you can breathe, you can give.

13.3 — The Four Levels of Morning Ṣadaqah

Not all ṣadaqah looks the same. Some is symbolic, some is substantial, some is invisible, and some costs nothing but intention.
Choose a level that matches your capacity each day — or rotate between them. What matters is consistency, sincerity, and showing up to Allah with a giving heart.

Level 1 — The £1/€1/$1 Habit

A symbolic daily seed.
Small in value, enormous in barakah.

This is the habit that trains your heart.
You give simply because you want Allah's pleasure at the start of your day. Tiny amounts done consistently carry spiritual weight far beyond their size.

Level 2 — The Weekly Investment

Once a week, choose a morning to give something meaningful:

- sponsor a meal
- support a masjid
- contribute to a widow or orphan fund
- plant a tree
- donate to a trusted charity
- support a da'wah initiative
- fund Qur'an education

These are heavier deeds that bring heavier barakah.
They become anchors in your week — moments of intentional generosity.

Level 3 — The Non-Monetary Morning

Ṣadaqah is not limited to money. The Prophet ﷺ taught:

> *"Every good deed is charity."*
> — Al-Bukhari

Begin your morning with acts that cost nothing but brighten someone's day:

- send a motivational voice note
- help a colleague without being asked
- reply with gentleness instead of irritation
- teach one beneficial thing
- uplift someone who is struggling
- make du'ā' for a friend in private

These forms of charity soften the heart and expand your compassion.

Level 4 — The Hidden Ṣadaqah

These are the deeds done quietly, anonymously, with no expectation of being seen or praised.

They are the hardest — and the most beloved to Allah.

A small, hidden act can outweigh a large public one.
They build sincerity, break ego, and draw you closer to Allah in ways no one else will ever witness.

When you vary your ṣadaqah levels, you train your heart to give in every season, every mood, every circumstance. And a heart that gives in the morning is a heart that walks through the day with barakah.

13.4 — The Connection Between Sadaqah and Rizq

The link between charity and provision is not symbolic — it is Qur'ānic.

Allah makes a direct promise:

> *"Whatever you give in charity, He will replace it."*
>
> *— Qur'ān 34:39*

Not "He *might*" replace it.
Not "He *could*" replace it.
He will.

This divine guarantee means your giving is never a loss — it is an investment. But Allah's replacement doesn't always arrive in the form you expect. His gifts come in the ways your life actually needs:
Protection from harm you never saw.
Calmness in moments that should have shaken you.
Unexpected clients or opportunities.
Ease in negotiations and decision-making.
Clarity that saves you from costly mistakes.
Doors opening where none existed.
Disasters quietly diverted before they reached you.
Healing in strained relationships.
A lightness in your day that money cannot buy.

Ṣadaqah invites rizq because it aligns your heart with generosity, trust, and sincerity — and Allah gives most abundantly to those who give.

When you give **in the morning**, you activate this divine cycle at the start of your day. You sow early so Allah can bring barakah into every hour that follows.

13.5 — The Sadaqah Mindset

Ṣadaqah is not only an action — it is a mindset.
It is a way of approaching life with generosity, trust, and clarity about where your provision truly comes from. When your heart gives with the right mindset, even the smallest charity becomes heavy in the scales.

Here is how to cultivate the mindset the Prophet ﷺ embodied.

Give intentionally

Begin your morning giving with purpose, not habit.
Let your heart speak as your hand gives:
"Yā Allah, I give for Your sake. Place barakah in my day, my work, and my decisions."

Intention transforms a small act into a spiritual investment.

Give quietly

Hidden ṣadaqah polishes the heart.
It uproots ego, weakens the desire for praise, and strengthens sincerity.

The deeds no one knows about are often the ones Allah loves most.

Give consistently

The Prophet ﷺ taught that *Allah loves consistent deeds*, even if they are small.
A pound a day, a message of kindness each morning, one helpful act — done regularly — nourishes the soul more than occasional large donations.

Consistency builds a giving heart.

Give with trust

Every act of charity is a declaration of faith:

"My wealth comes from Allah, not my hands."
"When I give, He replenishes."
"When I release, He replaces."

Ṣadaqah reminds you that Allah, not your effort, is the true Provider.

The sadaqah mindset shifts your entire day:
you start with generosity, walk with trust, and end with gratitude.

13.6 — Real-Life Morning Sadaqah Routines

Morning ṣadaqah is not abstract — it is practical, simple, and woven into real life.
Whatever your role, your responsibilities, or your financial situation, you can begin your day with charity that opens doors and brings barakah into your hours.

Here are examples of small, realistic routines for different walks of life. Use them as inspiration, not limitation.

The Entrepreneur
Begin your morning with generosity that matches your mission:

- Donate £1 each morning — a symbolic but powerful seed.
- Share one genuinely useful resource with your audience.
- Leave a supportive comment for someone building something meaningful.

The heart that builds others is the heart Allah builds.

The Student
Your knowledge is a form of charity:

- Share class notes with sincerity.
- Help someone understand a difficult concept.
- Make du'ā' for a friend who is overwhelmed.

Every act of support multiplies your own barakah in learning.

The Parent

Your home is your first charity field:

- Give your child attentive presence — it is one of the greatest forms of sadaqah.
- Speak gently in the morning, even when tired.
- Give a small charity on behalf of your children.

Mercy in the home is a sadaqah that shapes generations.

The Professional

Generosity elevates your workplace:

- Encourage a colleague who seems stressed.
- Offer brief mentorship or guidance.
- Buy someone a coffee with a kind intention.

A supportive environment is created through small, intentional acts.

The Homemaker

Your service carries enormous reward:

- Prepare something for the family with the intention of sadaqah.
- Make du'ā' for your home's peace and protection.
- Send a comforting reminder to someone who needs it.

Your unseen acts are seen by Allah.

The One Struggling Financially

You are not excluded from charity — you are its closest companion.

- Du'ā' is sadaqah.
- Smiling is sadaqah.
- Patience is sadaqah.
- Restraining anger is sadaqah.

Allah never restricts charity to money.
As long as you can breathe, you can give.

Everyone can give — and the morning is the best place to begin.

13.7 — The "Morning Ṣadaqah Box" Method

A Small Box That Rewires the Heart

If you want one habit that quietly transforms your relationship with wealth, discipline, and trust in Allah — this is it.

It is simple.
It is humble.
And it works.

How It Works

1. **Place a small box** near your prayer mat or Qur'ān stand.
2. **After Fajr**, drop a coin or £1 inside.
3. **At the end of the month**, give everything away for the sake of Allah.

That's it.
No complexity.
Just consistency.

What This Habit Teaches

Every morning when your hand reaches for that box, you're training your heart in four powerful qualities:

1. Consistency

You give before the day can distract you.
A believer who gives daily becomes a believer who remembers daily.

2. Discipline
You teach your nafs that generosity is not optional.
It is who you are.

3. Gratitude
You start the morning acknowledging that everything in your hand was placed there by Allah — not by effort.

4. Trust
You declare, silently:
"Yā Allah, You replace whatever is given for Your sake."

Few routines shape tawakkul as quickly as this one.

Why This Method Works So Well

A visible box near your prayer area becomes:
a trigger
a reminder
a training tool
a symbol of who you want to become

It turns giving into a *habit*, not a mood.

And if you have children, this becomes one of the most beautiful things they imitate. They watch you give every morning — and without instruction, their tiny hands follow yours.

This is how you plant generosity across generations.

13.8 — The Digital Barakah Method

Turn Your Online Presence into a Stream of Sadaqah

We live in a world where much of our influence, connection, and communication now happens online. That means your *digital life* is a space where reward can multiply — or where it can slip away unnoticed.

The believer who understands this treats their online presence as a **barakah engine**, not a distraction.

Morning is the best time to activate it.

How It Works

After Fajr — before the noise of the world reaches you — do **one digital act of khayr**:

- **Share a beneficial link** — *Islamic reminder, charity appeal, mental health support*
- **Uplift someone's work** — *small creators, students, entrepreneurs, masajid initiatives*
- **Send a sincere reminder** — *a du'ā', an āyāh, a phrase of hope*
- **Support a small Muslim business** — *a like, a comment, a share — all count*
- **Spread verified Islamic content** that brings reward long after you've logged out

Each action is small, but the ripple effect is enormous.

Why Digital Sadaqah Counts So Much

Because what you share online:
travels further than your voice

reaches hearts you will never meet
continues earning reward while you sleep
can uplift someone at a critical moment
can spark goodness for thousands

A single sincere post can become a **Sadaqah Jāriyah** (ongoing charity).

The Mindset Behind Digital Giving

Your intention turns ordinary online behaviour into extraordinary reward.

Say before posting or sharing:
"Yā Allah, make this a source of guidance and barakah for someone today."

This transforms:
scrolling into service
technology into ibādah
your presence into a means of goodness

A Morning Rule That Changes Everything

Never leave the online world without planting one seed of khayr.

If you do this daily, your digital footprint becomes a map of mercy — a trail of goodness that follows you into the next life.

Your online presence can be a sadaqah machine.
Use it with purpose.

13.9 — When You Need Something from Allah

When you're facing a closed door — an urgent need, an unexpected crisis, a breakthrough that feels out of reach — give ṣadaqah.

The scholars often say:

> *"When you need an urgent door to open, give ṣadaqah first."*

Ṣadaqah is spiritual leverage.
You are asking Allah while standing on an act **He loves** — an act that carries promise, protection, and reward.

You give, then you ask.
You plant, then you pray.
You offer something for His sake, and He opens what you cannot.

13.10 — Troubleshooting

Even the habit of giving has its challenges. Here is how to navigate them with ease and confidence.

"I keep forgetting."

Automate £30/month (or whatever you can) to a trusted charity.
Everything else you give becomes bonus barakah.

Automation builds consistency when the mind is busy.

"I feel insincere."

Sincerity grows *through* the action, not before it.
Keep giving — your heart will catch up with your hands.

"I don't see results."

Barakah is often invisible but deeply felt:

- protection
- avoided harm
- peaceful moments that should have been chaotic
- ease in the things that usually drain you
- relationships healing quietly
- guidance arriving at the right moment

Do not measure divine results with dunya metrics.

"I'm struggling financially."

Give something non-monetary.
A smile, a duʿāʾ, a helpful message, a patient silence — all of these count.

Allah does not ask you for your balance.
He asks you for your effort.

Ṣadaqah is not merely a charitable act —
it is **a barakah act**.

It cleanses what you earn.
It protects what you fear losing.
It expands what you already have.
It softens the hardness that builds in the heart.

A barakah-filled morning is not just about building *your* life —
it is about building *someone else's day*.

A believer is a giver, even when they have little,
because they know exactly **Who** is giving to them.

This is **Habit 9** —
the final pillar of the Barakah Morning,
the habit that opens doors in dunya
and builds palaces in Jannah.

When you give in the morning,
Allah writes generosity into the rest of your day.

CHAPTER 14

Conclusion — Living the Barakah

Morning, Every Day

A barakah-filled life doesn't happen by accident.

It is built — gently, consistently, intentionally — one dawn at a time.

When you began this journey, you were simply curious:
"What would my life look like if I actually lived a Sunnah morning?"

Now, you've seen what the early hours contain:

- clarity
- softness
- discipline
- spiritual alignment
- emotional stability
- creative focus
- divine assistance
- connection to Allah

The morning is not just a time of day.
It is a place where Allah distributes provision, opens doors, and invites His servants to draw nearer.

You now hold nine prophetic habits that change everything when practiced together:

1. Wake intentionally

2. Praise Allah
3. Glorify Allah
4. Recite Qur'ān
5. Send blessings on the Prophet ﷺ
6. Fulfil the morning adhkār
7. Pray Duḥā
8. Practice morning du'ā' and tawakkul
9. Give morning sadaqah

Each habit is powerful alone.
But together? They form a Barakah Operating System — a framework that shapes your identity, your energy, your decisions, your relationships, and your spiritual trajectory.

14.1 — What Actually Changes When You Live This Way

When you build your mornings on dhikr, Qur'ān, du'ā', and ṣadaqah, you don't just change your routine — you change your life from the inside out. The shifts may begin subtly, but they compound with extraordinary force.

Here is what starts to transform.

1. Your Mind Becomes Clearer

The noise of the world no longer enters your head before Allah does.
Your first thoughts are anchored, not scattered.
You begin the day knowing who your Lord is and who you are — everything else becomes easier to manage.

A clear morning produces a clear life.

2. Your Heart Grows Softer

Morning dhikr slows the ego.
Morning Qur'ān nourishes the soul.
Morning ṣadaqah purifies the intention.

You become less reactive, more patient, more aware of Allah, and more gentle with yourself and others. The spiritual armour you put on early protects your heart for the rest of the day.

3. Your Productivity Becomes Barakah-Based

You stop forcing outcomes.
You stop chasing results with desperation.
You work — but Allah is the One who grants success.

Doors open unexpectedly.
Assistance arrives from places you could never have planned.
Your effort is the same, but the *results* are different — because they are infused with barakah.

4. Your Stress Levels Drop

You no longer begin the day with urgency and panic.
You begin with remembrance — and remembrance reframes everything.

The emails feel lighter.
The problems feel solvable.
The day feels manageable.

A heart that starts with Allah is not easily shaken.

5. Your Identity Shifts

You stop seeing yourself as someone who is *trying* to be consistent.
You become someone who **is** consistent.

You become the type of person who wakes with purpose, who speaks to Allah before speaking to the world, who gives before receiving, who anchors the day in barakah instead of chaos.

That identity carries you — and it quietly transforms who you believe you can become.

Living this way doesn't just change your morning.
It changes your mind, your heart, your productivity, your stress, and your sense of self.
This is the power of a barakah-filled life.

14.2 — The Barakah Morning Is Not About Perfection

Not every morning will shimmer with focus.
Some mornings will feel strong and energised.
Some will be soft and quiet.
Some will be rushed.
Some will be messy and human.

And that is completely okay.

Allah does not ask you to be perfect.
He asks you to **try**, to **return**, and to keep your heart oriented toward Him. Your effort is worship. Your return is worship.

So, when you miss a habit:

- don't criticise yourself
- don't declare failure
- don't quit

Instead:

- restart that same evening
- ask Allah for strength
- take the next small, doable step

Consistency is built on returning, not on never slipping.

And remember the golden rule:

The Barakah Morning is won the night before.

When your night routine becomes scattered, your morning will reflect it. When your night is aligned — with dhikr, wind-down, intention, and rest — your morning rises with clarity and grace.

The goal isn't perfection.
The goal is a heart that keeps coming back to Allah, again and again, no matter how the morning looks.

14.3 — Your New Identity: A Morning Servant of Allah

By living the Barakah Morning, you have stepped into a new identity — a way of life rooted in *tawbah, dhikr, Qur'ān, discipline, presence, and generosity.*
This is no longer a routine.
It is who you are becoming.

A believer who rises early becomes someone who is:

- **spiritually awake** — the heart alive before the world stirs
- **emotionally stable** — grounded before the day tests you
- **mentally sharp** — focused because you began with clarity
- **protected and guided** — wrapped in the du'ā' of dawn

- **walking with divine help** — assisted in ways you cannot measure

When you stand before Allah in the quiet of dawn, you are making a declaration with your body, heart, and time:
"Yā Allah, You come first."

And when Allah comes first, everything else — your work, your family, your decisions, your path — falls into place with a beauty and ease you could never create on your own.

This is your new identity:
a morning servant of Allah — anchored, guided, elevated.

14.4 — Your 3 Non-Negotiables Going Forward

When life becomes heavy, chaotic, or overwhelming, these are the three pillars that will pull you back into alignment. No matter what slips, no matter what season you're in, hold onto these — they will revive your heart and stabilise your days.

1. Qur'ān in the Morning

Even **one āyah**.

Never let a morning pass without touching the Book of Allah — reciting it, reading its meaning, or allowing it to settle into your heart.
A single āyah can redirect an entire day.
A single āyah can reshape your outlook.
A single verse can nourish a tired soul.

This is your anchor of guidance.

2. Morning Adhkār

Your shield.
Your protection.
Your spiritual nourishment.

The morning adhkār place divine guards around your heart, your family, your work, and your day. These are not rituals — these are lifelines.
Even when everything else feels unstable, these words steady you.

3. Staying Awake After Fajr

This is the **anchor habit** — the one that stabilises all the others.

When you stay awake after Fajr, you honour the time that carries barakah.
You enter the morning the way the Prophet ﷺ taught.
Your mind, body, and heart align.
Your spiritual and worldly productivity rise together.

This single habit quietly disciplines your entire life.

These three are your non-negotiables.
When things fall apart, hold onto them.
They will revive you, refocus you, and reset your spiritual direction — every time.

14.5 — A Final Du'ā' for You

May Allah make your mornings filled with light — light that settles in your chest, guides your steps, and protects your path.

May He fill your heart with Qur'ān — āyat that anchor you, heal you, and accompany you through every season of life.

May He make dhikr sweet upon your tongue —
a comfort in hardship and a companion in ease.

May He grant you a consistency that even you did not believe you were capable of — a consistency that becomes your new identity.

May He unlock for you provision that arrives from places you never imagined — halal, pure, abundant, and full of barakah.

May He write you among the people of the dawn —
those He praises in the Qur'ān,
those who rise when others sleep,
those whose hearts He draws closest to Himself.

And may this book be a witness for you on the Day
when every minute of remembrance is counted,
every āyahrecited is elevated,
and every moment you fought sleep to worship Him
is multiplied in reward.

Āmīn.

CHAPTER 15

Identity Reset: Becoming the Person Who Lives This Lifestyle Consistently

"Allah does not change the condition of a people until they change what is within themselves."
— Qur'an 13:11

This chapter shifts the entire book from morning routine → life transformation. Because at some point, habits are not the issue. Identity is.

Most Muslims don't struggle because Fajr is too early, or Duḥā is too difficult, or dhikr is too much. They struggle because the *identity* they live with does not support the habits they aspire to.

If you do not upgrade the identity behind your routine, the routine eventually collapses.

This chapter rebuilds who you are internally so that the 9 habits become natural, automatic, and deeply rooted.

15.1 The Islamic Identity Framework: "Be Before You Do"

Modern self-help says:
change your actions → identity will follow.

Islam says:
change your intention, belief, and self-concept → your actions will align.

This is prophetic psychology:

> *"Actions are only by intentions."*

Meaning actions FLOW from internal states.

To become consistent, you must become the kind of person who naturally:

- values early mornings
- feels pulled toward Qur'an
- feels guilty missing Duḥā
- craves dhikr
- finds peace in duʿāʾ
- prefers remembrance over scrolling
- sees morning barakah as identity, not effort

You need to shift from:

> "I'm trying to build a good morning routine."
> to
> "I'm a believer who begins the day with Allah."

Identity produces automatic behaviour.

15.2 The 4 Levels of Islamic Identity

Your identity is built on four layers:

Level 1 — What You DO — *Your actions*

- Observe salat
- read Qur'an
- give sadaqah
- make dhikr

This is the surface level.

Level 2 — What You FEEL Responsible For — *Your values*

- "I value barakah."
- "I value waking early."
- "I value a heart connected to Allah."

Values strengthen consistency but are still emotional.

Level 3 — What You BELIEVE About Yourself — *Your self-concept*

- "I am someone who guards my Fajr."
- "I am someone who keeps my tongue moist with dhikr."
- "I am someone who begins their day with Allah no matter what."

This starts locking the behaviour into your identity.

Level 4 — Who You ARE Before Allah — *Your spiritual identity*
This is the deepest level.

Examples:

- "I am a servant of Allah."
- "I am a believer who seeks His pleasure."
- "I am someone who wants to meet Allah with a glowing record."
- "I am a person of morning barakah."
- "I am someone whom Allah loves to see rise early."

When you reach Level 4, the routine no longer feels like effort.
It feels like *you*.

15.3 The Biggest Identity Blockers

You cannot become consistent if you hold onto identities like:

❌ "I'm not a morning person."
Against prophetic instruction

❌ "I'm not disciplined."
Your nafs is lying. You are disciplined in what you care about.

❌ "I'm spiritually weak."
You're stronger than you think — the fact you are reading this proves it.

❌ "I keep failing."
Failure is part of identity formation.

❌ "My routine is ruined if I miss one day."
No. The Sahabah missed things. The strong believer returns quickly.

Every identity blocker must be dismantled with Qur'an, dhikr, and intention.

15.4 How to Build a Strong Islamic Identity — 5-Step Reset

This is where real transformation begins.

Step 1 — Name the Identity You Want to Become

Not vague.
Not "a better Muslim."

Something specific:

- "A believer who wakes at Fajr easily."

- "A Muslim whose heart is alive with Qur'an."
- "A person of morning barakah."
- "A worshipper who gives daily."
- "A believer with a purified tongue."

Write it as a statement of BEING, not DOING.

Step 2 — Attach Spiritual Meaning to That Identity

Answer this: *"Why does Allah love this version of me?"*

Examples:

- "Allah loves early risers."
- "Allah loves hearts connected to Qur'an."
- "Allah loves those who remember Him abundantly."
- "Allah loves those who give in the morning."
- "Allah loves those who trust Him at dawn."

When your identity becomes connected to Allah's love, it becomes magnetic.

Step 3 — Break the Old Identity with a Single Statement

Say quietly:
"I am no longer the person who delays Fajr / neglects Qur'an / begins the day in heedlessness."

This disrupts your old self-image.

Step 4 — Reinforce the New Identity with Tiny Wins

Identity is formed by evidence.

Examples:

- one page of Qur'an
- 10 salawāt
- 30 seconds of dhikr
- £1 sadaqah
- 2 rak'ahs of Duḥā

These micro-actions tell your brain: *"This is who I am now."*

Step 5 — Visualise the Believer You Want to Meet on the Day of Judgement

Not the successful version of you in dunya.
The *successful version in ākhirah.*

What does he/she look like?

- consistent
- calm
- glowing
- disciplined
- beloved to Allah
- anchored
- spiritually alive

This pulls your identity upward.

15.5 The Day You Become Consistent — Identity Integration

You know your identity has shifted when you start saying:

- "I feel off if I don't read Qur'an."
- "I don't feel right without Duḥā."
- "Dhikr feels natural now."

- "My morning feels empty without salawāt."
- "I can't imagine going back to sleeping after Fajr."

This is the goal.

Not perfection.
Not rigidity.
But consistency that feels like home.

15.6 Disruptions, Relapses, and 'Bad Days'

Even the companions had:

- off days
- missed opportunities
- spiritual dips
- emotional heaviness

A bad day is not failure.
The only failure is stopping.

Remember: *A disrupted routine is not a broken identity.*

Identity remains.
Habits resume.

The strong believer returns quickly.

15.7 The Dhikr of Identity

Say this every morning for 7 days:

"Yā Allah, make me among those who

begin their day with You,
live their day with You,
and end their day with You.
Make this my identity, not just my habit."

Then repeat:

يَا مُقَلِّبَ الْقُلُوْبِ ثَبِّتْ قَلْبِيْ عَلَىٰ دِيْنِكَ

"Yā Muqallib al-qulūb, thabbit qalbī ʿalā dīnik."
"O Turner of hearts, keep my heart firm upon Your religion."

This is the identity anchoring duʿāʾ.

15.8 Your New Identity Statement

Write yours, but here is a template:
"I am a believer who wakes early, remembers Allah abundantly, fills my heart with Qur'an, sends blessings on the Prophet ﷺ, trusts Allah deeply, gives generously, and walks the day with barakah."

Say it.
Believe it.
Live it.

This is the person Allah is shaping you into.

CHAPTER 16

Barakah-Based Productivity: Working with Allah, Not Just With Willpower

"if Allah helps you, no one can overcome you,"
— Qur'an 3:160

Worldly productivity worships energy, discipline, efficiency, and speed. But for a believer, productivity is not mechanical — it is spiritual.

Barakah is the competitive advantage no planner, no app, and no habit system can replicate.

It is a divine force that accelerates your work, protects your time, and multiplies your results in ways your effort alone never could.

This chapter transitions you from hustle-based productivity to **Allah-powered productivity** — a state where you accomplish more in three hours than many people achieve in a full day.
Where your work becomes lighter, your mind becomes clearer, and your time becomes a source of mercy, not pressure.

This is the mindset shift that will redefine how you work, how you plan, and how you measure success.

16.1 What Is "Barakah Productivity"?

Barakah is not speed.
Barakah is not urgency.
Barakah is not squeezing more tasks into fewer hours.

Barakah means:
Allah places goodness inside your time
Allah shields your time from waste
Allah multiplies the impact of your smallest effort
Allah removes obstacles before they ever reach you
Allah lightens what felt heavy ten minutes ago

You work less.
Allah makes it more.

That is barakah.

16.2 Why Willpower Alone Fails Most Muslims

You already know this from experience:

- Some days you're energised but achieve nothing.
- Some days you're exhausted but finish everything.
- Some days you're disciplined yet see no progress.
- Some days one small action unlocks the entire day.

This happens because **worldly productivity is horizontal** — it relies purely on human effort, optimisation, and planning.

Barakah productivity is vertical — it is assistance descending from Allah into your day.

When your time is aligned with Allah:

- clarity rises
- distractions fall
- focus becomes effortless
- anxiety softens

- decision-making becomes intuitive
- your heart becomes steady and unbothered

Because barakah is not a psychological hack — it is a spiritual technology.

16.3 The 7 Barakah Multipliers

These are factors that dramatically increase the blessings in your work.

You have already been building them in earlier chapters — now you will see how they directly supercharge your productivity.

1. Starting the Day With Allah — *Fajr* → *Duḥā*

The Prophet ﷺ made duʿāʾ:

> *"O Allah, bless my ummah in their early mornings."*

Barakah sits in the hours after Fajr.

When you work after Fajr:

- ideas are sharper
- concentration is higher
- Allah opens doors
- distractions are removed

Your brain is chemically wired for focus at dawn.
Your soul is spiritually wired for focus at dawn.

2. Dhikr That Sharpens the Mind

Dhikr — especially SubḥānAllāh, Alḥamdulillāh, Allāhu Akbar — clears your internal mental fog.

It is spiritual decluttering.

When your tongue remembers Allah, your mind stops remembering everything else.

3. Qur'ān Flow State

Qur'ān does not only calm you — it organises your cognitive bandwidth.

Studies show recitation patterns:

- stabilise breathing
- regulate heart rate
- reduce cortisol
- improve executive function

The result?
A calmer mind.
A calmer mind works faster.

4. Tawakkul — Trusting Allah with Outcomes

Worldly productivity:
"I must control everything."

Barakah productivity:
"I take action and leave results to Allah."

This removes anxiety — the #1 thief of focus.

A calm heart is a productive heart.

5. Sadaqah That Unblocks Rizq

The Prophet ﷺ taught:

"Sadaqah extinguishes calamities."

Calamities don't always look dramatic.
Sometimes they're:

- wasted hours
- blocked opportunities
- broken focus
- emotional heaviness
- unexpected delays
- demotivation
- minor crises that derail your day

Sadaqah clears your path.

6. Serving People

Serving others is a prophetic barakah magnet.

Help someone in the morning and watch:

- ease enter your work
- people respond to you better
- Allah place softness in your interactions
- doors open without pushing

Service purifies your niyyah —
purified intentions attract divine aid.

7. Avoiding Sins That Drain Barakah

You can have the best planner, the best desk, the best goals — but a single sin done casually can drain barakah for the entire day.

Sins bring:

- heaviness
- spiritual dullness
- laziness
- irritability
- distraction
- friction
- confusion

Guarding the eyes, ears, and tongue is a productivity strategy.

16.4 The Three Work Modes of a Muslim

A believer does not work the way the dunya works. Barakah-based productivity follows a divine rhythm — **three work modes that align your effort with how Allah designed the mind, the heart, and the day to flow.**

When you honour these modes, your time expands. When you violate them, your day becomes heavy.

Mode 1 — Deep Work — The Khulwah of Focus

Fajr → Duḥā

This is your highest-value window — the "barakah zone."

Use it for tasks that require:

- writing
- strategising

- planning
- learning
- problem-solving
- creative output

During this window:

- No phone.
- No social media.
- No casual chatting.
- No multitasking.
- No reactive tasks.

This is the period when Allah places blessing in your work.
Guard it with discipline.
Protect it like treasure.

Mode 2 — Light Work — *Maintenance Tasks*

After Duḥā / early afternoon, your brain shifts.
This time is ideal for:

- admin
- emails
- meetings
- scheduling
- logistics
- errands

These tasks do not require creative force — just consistency.

Mode 3 — Social Work — People-Facing Engagement

Late afternoon until Maghrib:

- collaboration
- family time
- helping others
- meetings that require emotional intelligence
- service
- community work

This is when your brain naturally moves into relational mode.

If you reverse these modes — you lose barakah and focus.

16.5 The Barakah-Based Workday — In Practice

> ***Seasonal Note:***
> *In winter months, the afternoon and evening windows compress as daylight shortens. This system does not demand equal hours — it honours divine order. When later windows shrink, priority naturally returns to the morning — and rest becomes an act of worship. Barakah is preserved not by extending effort, but by aligning with the season Allah has set.*

What follows is not a repetition of the work modes — it is their translation into a lived day.
The modes describe *how* barakah moves.
This shows *where* it anchored — anchored to the prayer cycle.

This is the daily architecture you have been building throughout the book: a structure aligned with revelation, human psychology, and the natural flow of barakah across the day.

It is not a schedule.
It is a *system* that harmonises your work with how Allah designed your mind, body, and soul to operate.

Fajr → Sunrise

Spiritual Activation Window

- Qur'ān
- Dhikr
- Du'ā'
- Planning your day
- Gentle reflection and grounding

This is your spiritual ignition — the reset that sets the tone for the next 24 hours.

Sunrise → Ẓuhr

The Barakah Work Block (Deep + Focused Execution)
This is the powerhouse of your day — the window where barakah, biology, and mental clarity align.

Use the early portion for:

- deep work
- strategy
- creativity
- planning
- learning

As your energy stabilises, transition naturally into:

- focused execution
- deliverables
- operational tasks
- implementation

No phones.
No notifications.
No reactive work.

A single protected morning block accomplishes more than a full day of scattered effort.

Ẓuhr → ʿAṣr

Meetings + Coordination Mode
This is where your social and relational bandwidth rises.

Best for:

- meetings
- teamwork
- collaborations
- customer-facing tasks
- decision-making with others

You're mentally responsive — not creatively drained, not emotionally flat.

ʿAṣr → Maghrib

Service, Family, & Light Productivity
Your day shifts into relational and physical mode.

Use this period for:

- family time
- community service
- errands
- movement

- light administrative tasks

This is the window where barakah enters through service and connection.

Maghrib → 'Ishā'

Calming Down + Spiritual Digestion
Your nervous system begins to soften.

This is the time for:

- unwinding
- spiritual reflection
- Qur'ān for the heart
- gratitude
- reviewing the day with gentleness

This window restores your inner balance.

After 'Ishā'

The Evening Shutdown Ritual

- close loops
- put the day to rest
- protect your sleep cycles
- prepare for the next dawn
- enter the night with calm, not chaos

A believer ends the day intentionally — because the next day begins from the night before.

16.6 How to Work with Allah, Not For the Work

This is the core shift that redefines your entire relationship with productivity:

❌ Working *FOR* the work

- stress
- pressure
- overthinking
- ego
- self-reliance
- exhaustion

✓ Working *WITH* Allah

- calm
- clarity
- flow
- consistency
- receptiveness
- divine support

A believer does not rely on willpower alone.
A believer relies on Allah at **every stage of the workflow**:

- **Before**: through niyyah
- **During**: through dhikr
- **After**: through shukr

This is how ordinary tasks transform into ongoing reward — and how effort feels lighter than expected.

16.7 — Dhikr That Accelerates Work — Practical Guide

Dhikr is not only spiritual nourishment — it is a practical productivity tool. Use specific adhkār as triggers throughout the day:

When overwhelmed:
"Ḥasbun Allāhu wa ni'ma al-Wakīl."
Allah is sufficient for us, and He is the best Disposer of affairs.

When stuck or out of ideas:
"Lā ḥawla wa lā quwwata illā billāh."
There is no power nor strength except with Allah.

When anxious before a meeting, call, or difficult task:
"Allāhumma yassir wa lā tu'assir."
O Allah, make it easy — do not make it hard.

When beginning a task:
"Bismillāh."
In the name of Allah,

When completing a task:
"Alḥamdulillāh."
All praise belongs to God

Dhikr aligns your heart and your effort — shifting you from tension to flow.

16.8 — The Niyyah Stack: Turning Every Task into Worship

Before you begin anything, silently affirm:
"Yā Allah, I do this seeking Your pleasure and halal provision."

Then add:
"Yā Allah, bless this work and protect my time from waste."

This is the **Niyyah Stack**:

- One intention for **dunya output**
- Another intention for **ākhirah reward**

You get double currency for the same action.
Your work becomes both productive and rewarded.

16.9 — Working From a State of Sakīnah

Sakīnah is divine tranquility — a calming weight of peace Allah places in the believer's chest.

Sakīnah:

- dissolves panic
- stabilises emotions
- enhances intuition
- improves decision-making
- strengthens discipline

You will feel sakīnah increasing when:

- Fajr becomes consistent
- Qur'an becomes daily
- Dhikr becomes second nature
- Duḥā becomes a habit
- Sadaqah becomes routine

A calm heart produces superior work.
A tranquil heart invites divine help.

16.10 — The Barakah Review — End-of-Day Check-In

At the end of the day, ask yourself:

- Did I begin with Allah?

- Did I trust Allah during my work?
- Did I remember Him at moments of difficulty?
- Did I end with gratitude?

The more "yes" answers you accumulate,
the more naturally barakah will flow in your time, work, and life.

This review takes one minute — but it transforms the next 24 hours.

16.11 — The Promise of Barakah

When your work aligns with Allah:
your time stretches
your mind sharpens
your heart softens
your work becomes worship
your rizq finds you
your soul stays protected
your ambitions become purified

This is not theory.
This is not motivational language.

This is a spiritual law witnessed by generations of believers before you.
Allah never allows His servant to lose when they work with Him.

CHAPTER 17

The Jumuʿah Reset System: Your Weekly Barakah Review

"The best day on which the sun has risen is Friday;"
— Sahih Muslim

Daily routines transform your mornings.
Weekly routines transform your entire trajectory.

Jumuʿah is not simply a prayer you attend once a week.
It is a divinely scheduled reset point — a built-in system for:

- recalibrating your intentions
- reviewing your progress
- cleansing your sins
- sharpening your īmān
- restoring discipline
- rebuilding momentum

This chapter gives you a **Friday operating system** that strengthens your spiritual core, stabilises your habits, and aligns you with barakah for the entire week.

This is your **weekly spiritual audit** — your **"barakah performance review."**

17.1 — Why Friday Is the Ultimate Reset Day

The Prophet ﷺ said:

"The best day the sun rises upon is Friday..."
— Muslim

Why is Friday the pinnacle of the week?

Because it carries:

- forgiveness
- answered du'ā'
- increased angelic presence
- a blessed hour guaranteed for acceptance
- renewal of īmān
- multiplication of reward
- heightened mercy
- greater spiritual sensitivity

Friday behaves like a mini-Ramadan every single week.

It wipes your slate clean.
It lifts your heart.
It repositions you for the next seven days.

From a productivity perspective, Jumu'ah is a built-in alignment mechanism:

- you reflect
- you realign
- you adjust
- you re-commit
- you elevate

When you use Friday intentionally, you protect yourself from drifting, dullness, and spiritual stagnation.

Jumu'ah resets your soul,
so your habits reset themselves.

17.2 The Friday Barakah Model

The Jumu'ah Reset System stands on **three pillars**, each designed to realign a different dimension of your life:

1. Spiritual Reset

Cleansing the heart + reconnecting with Allah.

2. Practical Reset

Reviewing your progress + recalibrating your week.

3. Emotional Reset

Releasing stress + resolving heaviness + repairing relationships.

Master these three pillars and **consistency becomes effortless**, because your heart, your habits, and your workflow are realigned every single week.

17.3 Pillar 1 — The Spiritual Reset

This is the soul of Jumu'ah.
Friday is the day your heart remembers *why* it works, *who* it works for, and *where* it is going.

1. Ghusl & Cleanliness — Entering a New State

The Prophet ﷺ emphasised:

- ghusl
- neat appearance

- clean clothing
- good scent

This is symbolic rebirth — a spiritual "new page."
You enter the day prepared, elevated, and ready for divine attention.

2. Surah al-Kahf — Light for the Week

The Prophet ﷺ said:

> *"Whoever recites Surah al-Kahf on Friday, a light will shine for him between the two Fridays."*
>
> — al-Ḥākim

This "light" is:
guidance
clarity
protection from confusion
strength in times of fitan

Surah al-Kahf resets your thinking and recentre your worldview.

3. Abundant Ṣalawāt on the Prophet ﷺ

On Fridays, your salutations reach him directly.

Every ṣalawāt is:
reward
purification
relief from hardship
du'ā' answered
sins erased

Friday is your weekly opportunity to increase it with intentionality.

4. The Hour of Response — Your Weekly Du'ā' Appointment

There is a hidden hour on Friday during which Allah **never rejects du'ā'**.

Most scholars say it falls **between 'Aṣr and Maghrib**.

Present everything:

- your dreams
- your fears
- your debts
- your projects
- your children
- your marriage
- your health
- your ākhira

This becomes your weekly **divine strategy session**.

5. Jumu'ah Prayer — Recentring the Heart

Jumu'ah is the ummah's weekly gathering — a moment where:
sins fall
hearts soften
guidance descends
remembrance elevates you

Your week is recentred in one khutbah.

17.4 Pillar 2 — The Practical Reset

Friday is your barakah-based productivity review.

This is where you measure your growth, remove friction, and adjust without guilt.

This review is not about judgment.
It is about realignment.

Every Friday, you will walk through the following five checkpoints.

A. Weekly Qur'ān Review

Ask yourself:

- How many pages did I recite?
- Did I recite consistently?
- Is there an ayah I want to focus on next week?

A believer treats Qur'an like nutrition — not an occasional supplement, and never optional.

B. Habits Consistency Check — *Attendance*

Rate each habit for the week:

- Stayed awake after Fajr
- Morning praise
- Tasbīḥ
- Qur'ān
- Ṣalawāt
- Du'ā' + Tawakkul
- Duḥā prayer
- Sadaqah
- Serving others

Use simple grading: Completed / Partial / Missed.

No guilt. Just awareness.
Awareness improves action.

Consistency opens the **doorway of barakah**.

C. Habits Alignment Score — *Quality & Presence*

After consistency, you assess quality.

This review answers a different question:
How did I show up?

For each habit, choose the description that best reflects your state during the week:

- Aligned — performed with presence, sincerity, and calm
- Mechanical — done, but rushed, distracted, or reduced to routine
- Resisted — marked by internal friction or heaviness
- Neglected — consistently avoided or abandoned

Consistency establishes structure.
Alignment determines how deeply barakah enters.

This step prevents habits from becoming hollow routines.

D. Work & Productivity Review

Ask:

- What drained barakah this week?
- What brought barakah?
- What tasks wasted time?
- What tasks produced high return?

This is how you evolve your workflow instead of repeating the same tired patterns.

E. Emotional & Mental Review

Ask:

- What stressed me this week?
- Where did I overcommit?
- What conversations remain unresolved?
- What did I avoid that needs attention?

Unchecked emotional weight quietly leaks barakah.
This review seals those cracks.

F. Planning the Next Week

Plan intentionally:

- Three major goals
- Qur'ān focus
- Sadaqah plan
- Du'ā' focus
- Family time
- Tasks to eliminate

You are not planning for busyness.
You are planning for clarity, sustainability, and barakah.

17.5 Pillar 3 — The Emotional Reset

This is the most underrated aspect.

Jumu'ah is your emotional detox.

1. Forgiveness Ritual

Say before Maghrib:

> *"Yā Allah, I release anyone who wronged me this week.*
> *Grant me a heart that You love."*

This protects your chest from corruption.

2. Repair One Relationship

Every Friday, reconnect with:

- a parent
- a sibling
- a friend
- a neighbour
- someone you drifted from

Relationships affect barakah.

Repairing relationships opens doors that effort alone cannot.

3. Treat Yourself Gently

Friday is a day of:

- softness
- mercy
- healing
- slowing down

Have tea.
Take a walk.
Rest.
Breathe.
Unclench the mind.

You cannot sustain high output without emotional release.

17.6 The Jumuʿah Reset Checklist (Simple + Practical)

Before Jumuʿah:

- Ghusl
- Clean clothes
- Qur'ān recitation
- Surah al-Kahf
- Ṣalawāt
- Duʿāʾ preparation

After Jumuʿah:

- Light meal
- Self-reflection
- Weekly habit review
- Qur'ān consistency check
- Productivity review
- Next week's plan

Before Maghrib — *Response Hour:*

- Make heartfelt duʿāʾ
- Forgive anyone who wronged you
- Ask Allah to bless your upcoming week

17.7 The Result of a Weekly Reset

If you perform the Jumuʿah Reset consistently:

- your week becomes structured
- your emotions become stable

- your habits become automatic
- your Duḥā and Fajr become easier
- your heart stays polished
- your rizq flow improves
- your spiritual resilience increases

Why?

Because a believer who checks in weekly with Allah never drifts too far.

CHAPTER 18

Your 30-Day Transformation Plan

"The most beloved actions to Allah are those done consistently, even if small."
— *Sahih al-Bukhari*

This is the chapter where everything becomes practical, structured, trackable, and achievable.

Up to now, you've learned the philosophy, the habits, the routines, the mindset, the identity, and the spiritual science behind morning barakah.

Now you convert all of that into a day-by-day system designed to transform your life in 30 days — gently, sustainably, and in a way that feels deeply Islamic, not overwhelming.

This is not a motivational challenge.
This is a reset of how you live your days.

The plan builds gradually:

- Week 1 → Foundation
- Week 2 → Activation
- Week 3 → Expansion
- Week 4 → Integration

By the end, you don't "try" this routine anymore.
It becomes who you are.

18.1 The Strategy Behind the 30-Day Plan — Why It Works

Most people fail because they try to change too much, too fast.

This plan is different.
It activates your transformation through four principles:

1. Micro-commitments
Tiny actions you cannot fail at.

2. Barakah timing
Habits stacked in the periods Allah blessed.

3. Identity reinforcement
You act like the person you want to become.

4. Spiritual momentum
Each day builds on the previous one, multiplying reward and motivation.

You're not forcing change.
You're allowing change.

A Note on Time
The weeks in this plan are not deadlines.
They are stages of formation.
Some readers will move through a stage in seven days.
Others may need two or three weeks — or longer.
That is not failure. That is honesty.
Barakah does not respond to speed.
It responds to sincerity and steadiness.
If Week 1 takes you three weeks, remain there.
Do not advance until the foundation feels settled.
This plan is designed to meet you where you are — not rush you where you are not ready to be.

18.2 Week 1: Foundation — "Anchor the Dawn"

The goal of Week 1 is not perfection.
It's simply to *wake up and meet the morning.*

You will build only THREE habits this week.

Do not move on because the calendar says so.
Move on when the habit feels natural.

Week 1 Habits

1. Stay awake after Fajr (even 10–15 minutes)
2. Morning praise (Alhamdulillāh)
3. Simple Qur'ān recitation (1–2 pages)

Everything else is optional.

Day 1–3: Orientation

- Wake up for Fajr
- Stay awake for at least 10 minutes
- Say "Alhamdulillāh" with presence
- Recite a minimum of one page
- One du'ā':
  "Yā Allah, bless my morning and make it a source of barakah."

Slow. Gentle. Easy.

Day 4–5: Stabilisation

- Try staying awake 20–25 minutes
- Read 2 pages
- Establish a fixed space

- Remove phone from bedroom
- Sleep slightly earlier

Your body begins adjusting.

Day 6–7: Confidence

- Stay awake 30 minutes
- Recite 3–4 pages
- Make a short du'ā' for your day's goals
- Reflect on how different you feel

End of Week 1:
Your mornings are now anchored.
Your day no longer starts in chaos.

18.3 Week 2: Activation — "Let the Heart Wake Up"

Now that your mornings are stable, add three more habits.

Week 2 Habits

4. Tasbīḥ (SubḥānAllāh)
5. Ṣalawāt
6. Du'ā' + Tawakkul

This week focuses on emotional awakening — clearing your chest, softening your heart, and strengthening tawakkul.

Daily Routine for Week 2

Right after Fajr:

1. Praise (Alhamdulillāh)
2. Tasbīḥ — 33× SubḥānAllāh

3. Ṣalawāt — 10×
4. Qur'ān — 2–4 pages
5. Du'ā' for the day:
   "Yā Allah, I rely on You. Replace my fear with calm and my effort with Your support."

You will feel:

- reduced morning anxiety
- increased clarity
- emotional stability
- stronger connection to Allah

By the end of Week 2:
Your heart wakes up *before the world touches you.*

18.4 Week 3: Expansion — "Move into Action"

This week adds two practical habits.

Week 3 Habits

7. Pray Duḥā
8. Daily sadaqah (even £0.20)

Duḥā opens doors.
Sadaqah removes obstacles.

This is the week your days start flowing beautifully.

Daily Plan for Week 3

Morning (post-Fajr):

- Praise
- Tasbīḥ
- Ṣalawāt
- Qur'ān
- Duʿāʾ
- Stay awake minimum 30–45 minutes

Mid-morning (sunrise + 15 minutes → before Ẓuhr):

- Duḥā (2 rakʿahs minimum)
- Give sadaqah (manual or automated)

This is where barakah in your rizq strengthens.
Work feels lighter.
You feel helped.

By the end of Week 3:
You experience support from Allah you did not feel before.

18.5 WEEK 4: INTEGRATION — "Become the Person of Morning Barakah"

This is the week of consolidation.

Week 4 Habit

9. Serving and helping others
   — small, simple, daily.

This can be:

- sending a kind message
- helping a family member
- listening attentively

- feeding birds
- supporting a neighbour
- sharing useful knowledge
- uplifting someone

The goal is to turn outward — to reflect barakah onto others.

Daily Plan for Week 4

Morning Ritual:

- All 9 habits
- Minimal screen time
- Dedicated 45–60 minutes for reflection or planning

During the day:

- Choose ONE act of service
- Make du'ā' for three people
- Offer help proactively
- Spread light everywhere you go

By the end of Week 4:
You no longer "try" to be consistent.
You are simply a person whose day begins with Allah.

18.6 The Weekly Layout (Quick Summary)

Week 1:
Anchor your Fajr and Qur'ān.
Week 2:
Awaken your heart with dhikr and du'ā'.
Week 3:
Open your rizq and momentum with Duḥā & sadaqah.

Week 4:
Transform your identity through service.

This is deliberate, structured spiritual engineering.

18.7 The 30-Day Transformation Checklist

Every day:

- Fajr
- Stay awake
- Praise
- Tasbīḥ
- Ṣalawāt
- Qur'ān
- Du'ā'
- Duḥā
- Sadaqah
- Service

Yes — it becomes easy.
Yes — it becomes automatic.
Yes — it becomes who you are.

18.8 The Promise of 30 Days

If you follow this plan:

- Your mornings will feel sacred
- Your mind will become clear
- Your heart will soften
- Your anxiety will reduce
- Your productivity will increase

- Your relationship with Allah will become intimate
- Your decisions will become guided
- Your life will move with barakah
- You will feel protected
- You will feel helped
- You will feel carried

Because Allah does not leave the one who rises early for His sake.

If you're ready, lets move into the final stage.

CHAPTER 19

The Lifelong Barakah Lifestyle

"Remain steadfast, as you have been commanded."

— Sūrah Hūd Q11:112

A true transformation is not created in a week or a month — it's built through small, steady acts that embed themselves into your identity until they become simply: *your way of living*.

This chapter is your transition from "I completed the 30-day plan" to:

"This is who I am now."

Here, you learn how to protect the habits you've built, deepen them, pass them on, and weave barakah into the seasons and decades of your life.

This is not about perfection.
This is about permanence.

This is the barakah lifestyle.

19.1 What It Means to Live with Barakah

Barakah living is defined by four qualities:

1. You begin your day with Allah

Every day starts on a spiritual foundation.

2. You work with Allah's help, not against your limits

Your effort is supported, guided, and opened by Him.

3. You protect your heart throughout the day

You guard your tongue, your eyes, your emotions.

4. You return to Allah each night

You close your day with reflection, forgiveness, and gratitude.

When this becomes your rhythm, your life feels:

- meaningful
- gentle
- calm
- guided
- consistent
- spiritually alive

This is not the "hustle life."
This is the *barakah life.*

19.2 The "Barakah Operating System" (BOS)

A lifelong barakah lifestyle runs on a simple internal system:

BOS = Morning Barakah + Daily Dhikr + Weekly Reset + Seasonal Renewal

Let's break that down.

1. Morning Barakah —*Daily Engine*

Your morning routine is the engine of your day.
You don't need to be perfect — you just need to show up.

Even when:

- you're tired
- you overslept
- life is chaotic
- kids are loud
- deadlines are heavy

Your minimum barakah pulse stays intact:

- Fajr
- Praise
- Qur'ān (even half a page)
- Salawāt (10× minimum)
- Dhikr (3 minutes)

This keeps your heart alive.

2. Daily Dhikr — Heart Maintenance

Dhikr is how you keep your internal system polished.

Throughout the day:

- SubḥānAllāh
- Alḥamdulillāh
- Allāhu Akbar
- Lā ilāha illā Allāh
- Lā ḥawla wa lā quwwata illā billāh

Small, quiet, continuous.

You don't need a tasbīḥ counter.
Your tongue becomes your tasbīḥ counter.

3. Weekly Reset — Jumu'ah System

You already built this in Chapter 17.

This weekly audit prevents:

- slippage
- emotional heaviness
- spiritual erosion
- loss of momentum

It realigns you *every single week.*

4. Seasonal Renewal — *Every 90 Days*

Every three months:

- refresh goals
- reset Qur'ān pace
- revisit du'ā' list
- evaluate habits
- eliminate distractions
- add one new act of worship
- recommit to service

This ensures you grow with intention, not drift with time.

19.3 When Life Gets Busy, Chaotic, or Hard

The barakah lifestyle is gentle.
It's flexible.
It's humane.

On difficult days, your routine shrinks to the essentials:

The "Minimal Barakah Formula"

- Fajr
- 60 seconds of praise
- 1 page Qur'ān
- 10 salawāt
- 1 act of kindness
- Sleep early

This maintains spiritual continuity without pressure.

Remember:
A believer never drops to zero.

19.4 Avoiding the Five Barakah Killers

To live with barakah long term, protect yourself from:

1. Sin done casually
Sins drain light and bring heaviness.

2. Chronic busyness
If everything is important, nothing is.

3. Scrolling without purpose
Mindless input poisons the heart and kills focus.

4. Sleeping late for no reason
A night with no discipline becomes a morning with no barakah.

5. Emotional grudges
Nothing suffocates barakah like an unhealed heart.

When barakah leaves, everything becomes harder.
When barakah returns, everything becomes easier.

19.5 The "Barakah Mindset" for the Decades Ahead

A lifelong barakah lifestyle rests on five mental anchors:

1. Long-term gentleness

You treat yourself with mercy.
You improve slowly.
You grow patiently.

2. Always returning

If you slip, you return.
If you fall, you return.
If you drift, you return.

Your relationship with Allah is defined by returning, not perfection.

3. Worship as identity

You no longer "do" the habits.
You *are* the kind of person who lives them.

4. Barakah is earned privately

The world sees your actions.
Allah sees your sincerity.

The hidden sincerity is what creates visible barakah.

5. Allah is the source of your strength

Your progress is not your achievement.
It is His generosity.

This keeps your heart humble, soft, and open.

19.6 Raising a Family with Barakah

Barakah is not individual — it's generational.

Your consistency becomes:

- your children's memories
- your grandchildren's inheritance
- your family's spiritual culture

Model the morning barakah rhythm in your home:

- gentle Qur'ān playing
- du'ā' aloud
- dhikr woven into everyday tasks
- family gratitude circles
- sadaqah boxes
- visiting neighbours
- forgiving quickly

Your home becomes a place where angels feel welcome.

19.7 Your Legacy: Becoming a Person of Dawn

There are believers whose faces shine on the Day of Judgement because:
— *I pray Allah make you one of them.*

- they guarded Fajr
- they recited Qur'ān consistently

- they remembered Allah in the quiet hours
- they served people
- they gave in the morning
- they trusted Allah with their day

You are becoming one of those believers.

A person of dawn.
A person of light.
A person whose entire life carries barakah.

19.8 The Prayer for a Lifelong Barakah Life

Say this often:

"Yā Allah, make my life a life of barakah.
Make my mornings pure, my heart sincere,
my actions consistent,
my worship accepted,
and my ending beautiful.
Let me live as a person of dawn
and meet You with a radiant face."

Āmīn.

19.9 The Journey Continues

You've reached the end of the written book —
but the transformation is only beginning.

You now hold:

- the habits
- the routines

- the identity
- the duʿāʾ
- the psychology
- the framework
- the system
- the barakah blueprint

This is your new life.

A life of dawn.
A life of light.
A life of purpose.
A life in which Allah walks with you through every day and every night.

Your journey continues — beautifully, quietly, consistently — in the presence of Allah.

Closing Message

A final reminder, a spiritual nudge, and a call to action.

As you close this book, remember that real transformation doesn't happen in big dramatic gestures. It happens through small, consistent acts done sincerely for Allah.

A minute of dhikr counts.
A single page of Qur'ān counts.
Ten salawāt count.
Two rakʿah Duḥā count.
A £1 charity counts.
A kind word counts.

A forgiving heart counts.
A quiet moment asking Allah for help counts.

Every sunrise is a fresh invitation from Allah:
"Start again. Come back. I am with you."

So, begin.
Begin imperfectly if you must.
Begin tired.
Begin busy.
Begin with shaky consistency.

But begin —
and watch how Allah carries you the rest of the way.

O Allah, bless every reader, strengthen their mornings, lighten their burdens, and pour barakah into their days. Grant them clarity, peace, and nearness to You.

Āmīn.

Thank you for journeying through these pages.
May Allah make every morning of your life a doorway to blessings you can feel, see, and live.

Railu Mustapha-Tiamiyu